Surviving Depression

My Agonizing Struggle
with Sanity

Robert L. Hamlett

VANTAGE PRESS
New York

FIRST EDITION

All rights reserved, including the right of reproduction in whole or in part in any form.

Copyright © 2008 by Robert L. Hamlett

Published by Vantage Press, Inc.
419 Park Ave. South, New York, NY 10016

Manufactured in the United States of America
ISBN: 978-0-533-15904-8

Library of Congress Catalog Card No.: 2007906603

0 9 8 7 6 5 4 3 2 1

To Dr. Steven Nyquist, the psychiatrist who helped free my mind, and to the untold numbers of persons struggling with depression. May my experience give those suffering from depression a ray of hope and the resolve to seek professional help.

Contents

Introduction ix

1. The Early Years
Owen Street 1
My Maternal Grandparents 3
My Parents 5
Morton Avenue 6

2. Adolescence
Innocence of Youth 8
My Dark Side 10
My Religious Upbringing 11
Emotional Trauma 12
A Family Tragedy 14

3. Puberty
Joining the "Big Boys" 17
Sixteen, at Last 19
Out of My Shell 20
Preparing for College 22

4. Coming of Age
Adapting to College Life 25
"Meltdown" 27
Finishing College 33
At Last, Love 39

5. Military Service
    Navy Officer Candidate School   42
    Navy Supply Corps School   47
    Lost Summer   50
    USS *Frontier*   57
    Vietnam   64

6. Transition to Civilian Life
    Exploring Asia   73
    Facing the Future   79
    Falling Apart   81
    Escape to Nowhere   85

7. Psychiatric Hospital
    Hopeless Souls   89
    Mother Teresa   91

8. Starting Over
    Job Search   96
    High School Reunion   100

9. The '70s
    Found My Calling   103
    Looking for Love   109
    Starting a Family   111
    Devil or Angel   115
    Test of Character   119
    The Good Life   128

10. Life Comes Unglued
    Feet of Clay   132
    Prelude to Disaster   133

Decision Time	136
Descent into Hell	138
A New Day	141

Epilogue   145

Introduction

I was born June 13, 1943. My life really began in April 1982, at the age of thirty-nine, when at long last I escaped the horrors of depression which had haunted me since birth. Upon first reflection, this account of my battle with depression might, in itself, seem negative and depressing. That is not my intention. When viewed with the proper perspective, it should be uplifting and give hope to the untold numbers attempting to survive this malady. This book, for the most part, covers only the first thirty-nine years of my life, which was a never-ending battle with depression and a struggle for my sanity. I will, however, include an epilogue to bring the reader up to date on what has transpired in my life since 1982.

I was born in the '40s, grew up in the '50s and reached manhood in the '60s. Doctors in those eras were just beginning to come to terms with the causes of depression and its debilitating effect. At that time, medication to treat depression was primarily experimental in nature and not available to most people. Depressed people, for the most part, had to struggle through life the best they could.

Before the advent of effective antidepressant medications and meaningful therapy, many depressed people found the experience more than they could endure. I was one of the fortunate ones that somehow managed to cope and maintain, at least from outward appearances, some semblance of normalcy. Unfortunately, many afflicted with depression during that era were not so lucky, either committing suicide, being warehoused in institutions or roaming the streets in despair, incurring the wrath and disdain of society.

Today, there is hope for people suffering from depression. Doctors have learned a great deal about the causes and effects of depression. Had I been born in the '70s or '80s instead of the '40s, my life might have been much different and this book unnecessary. Unfortunately, today there remain untold numbers of depressed people in our society whose suffering goes undiagnosed and untreated. These are the people I hope to reach with this book.

Until I was hospitalized in 1969, at the age of twenty-six, not a single person was aware of the demons I had been fighting all my life. Even my family and friends were oblivious to the periods of hopelessness and despair that I had endured. From all appearances, I had led a "normal" life and, in some ways, appeared to be a high achiever. In high school, college, the military and in my later work experience, I managed to "muddle through" and to some extent excel. I had an instinct for survival which compelled me to endure life regardless of how painful it might be.

Most people probably do not understand how I could have survived and had the semblance of a normal life had I suffered constantly from depression. If the depression had been constant, I probably would have been an early casualty of the disease. In my experience, the depression "waxed and waned." I sometimes went months suffering only modest depression. There were even periods when the malady was dormant and I experienced the happiness that other people feel. However, I was constantly waiting for "the other shoe to fall." When it fell, it often did so with a vengeance.

There were several periods in my life which were devastating. I sometimes lost the ability to function. I retreated into the dark recesses of my own psyche. These episodes were sometimes brought about by traumatic events which "kicked in" the depressive episodes. At other times, depression ensued for no apparent reason. These episodes lasted from a few weeks to a few months, on occasion resulting in an extended stay in a psychiatric hospital. Sometimes with the help of medication, sometimes without, the depression eventually subsided and I was able to try to resume a "normal" life.

I sometimes wonder how I managed for so long to endure life's roller coaster ride, knowing that at any time my life might revert from relative normalcy to bewilderment, hopelessness and despair. A friend I had known since college recently reminded me of something I had often heard before.

"The trials and tribulations that don't kill you make you stronger."

1

The Early Years

Owen Street

My first recollections of life occurred while living with my parents and maternal grandparents on Owen Street in North Nashville, where we lived until I was almost six years of age. Our home was located across the street from North High School, from which my mother had recently graduated.

When the subject came up, my family always referred to us as "working class." In fact, although we always had the necessities of life, we were very poor and were very near, if not part of, the underclass of society. My mother and father were the only members of their respective families who had graduated from high school. To my family's credit, I never realized, until I was an adult, just how poor we were. Of course, there was no reason for me to question my lot in life since our neighbors on Owen Street and, later, on Morton Avenue, where we moved when I was very young, were of the same socio-economic status as our family. Having no contact with the people in the more affluent sections of Nashville, we had no idea how the "other half" lived.

My first remembrances of life on Owen Street are the nights when I would cross the street, press my face into the chain link fence surrounding North High School's football field, and be mesmerized by the action on the field. Perhaps, this was the beginning of my fascination with football, which I carry with me to this day. In fact, in my later years, I have become a "Fantasy Football Fanatic," which only those similarly enthralled can appreciate. Perhaps, a more telling predictor of my innate personality occurred even before I was old enough to recall the incident. It was recounted several times during my youth, usually followed by much laughter. Everyone but me still thinks the incident funny.

When I was about two years of age, Nashville was blanketed with several inches of snow. Looking out the window, I observed snow for the first time. As related by my family, I turned from the window aghast at developments. Apparently horrified at the prospect of being blamed for the incident, I assured my family, in fearful tones, that "somebody else did that." This was the first exhibition of a personality trait that I live with to this day. I tend to fear the worst in all situations, even when the fears are completely irrational and unfounded. Decades later, the psychiatrist who found a way to free my mind, described the phenomenon as "Seeing an Indian behind Every Tree." This personality trait has resulted in my being perpetually "on guard," lest disaster strike at any minute. That is no way to go through life.

The other vivid memory of my life on Owen Street is accompanying my father to the site on Morton Avenue, in South Nashville in an area known as "Flatrock," where my father, by himself, was building our future home. My father had a "real job" at Vultee Aircraft; however, he spent weekends and any other time he could spare, working on building our future home. Of course at my tender age, I was no help on the project. I guess he just liked me "tagging along."

Although my father had many shortcomings as a husband and father, as will be delineated later, he was a good provider to his family's physical, if not emotional, needs. By himself, he built our new home on Morton Avenue, from the foundation to the roof. The only outside help he obtained were the services of a brick layer and an electrician. Unfortunately, my father's innate abilities in construction were not passed down to me. When a teenager, I attempted to build a dog house for one of the many canine pets I had during my youth. Flabbergasted at my inability to accomplish such a rudimentary task, my father "bailed me out" and completed the project.

My Maternal Grandparents

I incurred many depressive episodes during the first thirty-nine years of my life. Although it has now been determined that a chemical imbalance is the primary culprit, my relationships and interaction with my family probably acerbated my mental problems. My family can be described, at best, as dysfunctional. One cannot understand my life experiences without taking into account my relationships with those closest to me. It is imperative that I give a brief synopsis of the four people with whom I was closest and those instrumental in forming the man I was to become.

My mother's father and mother lived with my parents and me on Owen Street and, later, on Morton Avenue. My relationship with my maternal grandparents was probably more of an influence on my psychological development than was that of my parents. My grandparents were born towards the end of the nineteenth century in Maury County in rural middle Tennessee. They were from poor farm families and married at an early age. They had quite a few children, several of whom died during childhood. Only five children reached adulthood. My mother was the youngest of the lot.

My grandfather, known as "Mr. Mac" (for McKennon), was forced to leave school after the second grade to help with the farm work on his father's farm. He never learned to effectively read or write although he could scan a newspaper and get a sense of what was happening in the world. Until his death, he signed his name with an "X." Although uneducated, he was a very wise, compassionate and honest man. Many of his "old sayings" concerning life were instrumental in me becoming the man into which I eventually evolved. At the time I did not understand their implications; however, when I reflected on them in later life I was inspired. Mr. Mac was a very good man. I loved him very much.

My grandmother, "Gertie" as she was known (short for Gertrude), was born with a serious handicap, one with which many people would have had difficulty overcoming. She was born without fingers. On each hand, were two small "stubs," with which she had to make do. Despite this handicap, she learned to do almost everything that people with fingers were able to accomplish.

Sometime in the 1920s, disdaining impoverished life on the farm, Mr. Mac and Gertie pulled up roots and moved their family to North Nashville. While my grandmother took care of the children, as was customary in those days, my grandfather got a manual job in a cement processing plant. Those were the days before environmental issues became a concern. His work there may have contributed to his health problems down the road. Despite his lack of education and his failure to effectively read and write, sometime in the '40s he left the cement plant and opened a small tavern in North Nashville, where he worked during the time we lived on Owen Street. Somehow, despite his limitations in communication, the tavern turned enough profit to sustain him and my grandmother. He retired about the time we all moved to Morton Avenue.

My Parents

My parents married when my mother was only eighteen, just out of high school, and my father was only twenty. Not quite nine months after they were married, I was born. Their marriage must have been a case of "raging hormones," for I can think of no other reason why they got married. They had little else in common. My mother, apparently, regretted almost immediately that she and my father had married. She told me shortly before her death that when I was only one year of age she had asked my father for a divorce. He responded that he would never give her a divorce. Apparently, she never asked again.

My parents stayed together over fifty-three years before my mother passed away in 1996. For many years, they managed to "get along" by leading almost separate lives. However, in the later years of their marriage, neither could hide their disdain, even hatred, for the other. It was truly a "marriage from hell." In 1992, they had the audacity to plan a celebration of their fifty years of marriage. I informed my mother that I would not attend, for, in my opinion, their marriage was nothing to celebrate. My mother was deeply hurt but said nothing. She knew I spoke the truth.

In spite of having three siblings, I was practically raised as an only child. I was almost nine years old when my sister Sandra was born. I am sixteen years older than my brother David and twenty-one years older than my brother Thomas. I am sure all of the births were "accidents." No person in their right mind would knowingly bring children into such a contentious environment.

Her marriage aside, my mother was loving and supportive during my formative years. I loved her dearly. Once we moved to Morton Avenue, the neighborhood children "hung out" at our house. My mother was somewhat of a "Pied Piper." Perhaps, she gave to her children and even to the neighborhood children, the love she neither gave nor received from her husband. Maybe, that is the only way she could make up for a loveless marriage and the emptiness in her own life.

Other than saying that he was a hardworking man who provided for the physical needs of his family, there is little complimentary that I can say about my father. My father was a self-absorbed, selfish, insensitive man who cared only for his own desires and needs. He was incapable of giving the love that his wife and children craved. Other than his poker and golf buddies, who only knew him superficially, he had no close friends. The most onerous aspect of my father's persona was a heart filled with hate. He hated blacks, Catholics, Jews and practically everyone else.

A boy normally adopts the values of his father, for his father is usually his role model. I must admit that, as a child, I "bought into" my father's view of those who were different. It was not until I was an adult and experienced the "real world," that I finally cast off the bonds of prejudice and bigotry. I have yet to forgive my father, even after his death, for the warped view of the world he taught me and my siblings.

Morton Avenue

After the house on Morton Avenue was finally completed in late 1948, plans were made for the big move. We finally moved, in the dead of winter, in January 1949. As it turned out, the timing of the move was fortuitous. Two days after the move, a winter storm, with several inches of accompanying snow and ice, inundated Nashville. There was no electricity for several days. Fortunately, we had a coal burning furnace and were not forced to move out of our house as did many others. However, it was an ominous beginning in a home that would know more than its share of unhappiness and tragedy.

2
Adolescence

Innocence of Youth

In the fall of 1949, I entered Turner Elementary School, within walking distance of our home on Morton Avenue. I had not gone to kindergarten, for in those times, kindergarten was not available for people of our social status. Overall, I was an excellent student and throughout elementary school, a favorite of my teachers. Most likely, I gained the teachers' favor primarily because, being introverted and very quiet, I was far less rambunctious than many of my classmates. During those early years, I did all the things that children in my social strata normally do. No one suspected the dark side of my nature. My parents, family, friends and others to whom I came into contact probably just considered me a "normal boy" who was quiet by nature. No one suspected the trauma of my existence, which I faced alone.

Practically every family in my neighborhood had one or more children roughly in my age group. The children with which I spent most of my hours participating in the games and fantasies of childhood were Enoch, Danny, Norma, Gayle, Billy Ray and Warren. Unlike today's generation of children who spend most of their time on the Internet, playing video games or watching television, we spent most of the time playing outside. In fact, when we first moved to Morton Avenue, television was unknown in our neighborhood.

We played kick the can, dodgeball, hide and seek, cops and robbers, cowboys and Indians, army, football, baseball, basketball and games we concocted ourselves. We even played a game which I later learned that, in less prejudiced parts of the country was called "monkey on the sidewalk." But, in the South, in the era of segregation and bigotry, the game had another name referring to black people in a derogatory manner.

Sometime during my elementary school years, the first television appeared in our neighborhood. Even though there was only one channel, no one, adults or children, seemed to care. Saturday morning, the kids would crowd around the television with their eyes glued on "Fury," Sky King," and the "Sealtest Big Top." In addition, my father put up a basketball goal in the backyard where, throughout my adolescence, I spent many hours. Ostensibly, I was honing my basketball skills. In fact, I liked the solitude where I could become lost in my own thoughts.

In the summer, I also often went to Coleman Park, which was about four blocks from my home. Enoch and I went daily to the small swimming pool in the park. In addition, on Saturdays, I would often go to the park alone to try to worm my way into the pickup baseball games which usually involved older boys. Unless they were shorthanded, I did not get to play. When I managed to secure a spot in the game, being younger, I was usually relegated to right field, often the placement for unskilled or inept players. Also, during the summer, my cousin Don, who was two years older, came to spend a couple of weeks with my family. It was good for Don because, even though my family's homelife left a lot to be desired, it was a step up over that to which he was accustomed. He fit right in with the neighborhood children who accepted him with open arms.

When I was about twelve years of age, the boys I knew began to have an interest in girls and sex. It is humorous when I recall all of the misinformation on the subject of sex we traded back and forth. We didn't have a clue. I sometimes slept over in Danny's home. The attraction was next door. The home next to Danny's was within a few feet of Danny's home. We soon discovered that Danny's bedroom window was right across from the teenage daughter's bedroom in the neighbor's home. Innocently, she would change into her bedclothes, often forgetting to pull down the shades. Even at twelve, the experience was very titillating.

My Dark Side

As one can see, from all appearances, I seemed like a typical young boy, being an excellent student and participating in all the activities usually associated with normal development. Appearances can be deceiving. I must discuss the things associated with my life that are contrary to what would be thought of as normal in the maturation process. In addition, I will reveal certain incidents in my life that played a part in my psychological development.

During my youth, I spent a great deal of time alone. This was by choice, as I was accepted by the neighborhood children and reasonably well liked. In fact, my mental state was often such that I lived in a world of my own, full of fears and anxieties about both the present and the future. My parents were aware that I spent a great deal of time alone. However, since I was a "good boy" and never caused my parents any trouble, they probably considered my temperament a good thing rather than something of which they should be concerned. Besides, they had enough issues in their marriage to preclude worrying about a son whose conduct appeared exemplary. They did not understand or contemplate the demons that dwelled beneath the surface of my soul.

As stated before in this book, my personality can best be exemplified as "Seeing an Indian behind every tree." I found myself brooding over every little event in my life, whether the threat to my existence was real or imagined. I often took offense, silently, at the actions of other people that I deemed threatening even though no such offense was intended. I tended to withdraw into a world of my own where no harm would come to me. During the many hours that I spent alone in my room, I invented many time-consuming games where I could replace the harmful realities of the world with a make-believe safe existence for which I yearned.

Perhaps the most bizarre and debilitating psychological problem I faced in my youth was an obsession with death. From the time I was a small child through my teenage years, I saw any minor abnormality, affliction or disease as impending doom. Many times I was sure I had a fatal disease and would not reach adulthood. I suffered in silence. Everyone, parents, teachers and playmates alike just thought me a normal quiet introverted boy. No one knew that I was a deeply disturbed young boy.

My Religious Upbringing

Religion was a contentious subject in our household. My mother had been born and reared a Methodist. My father and his family belonged to the Church of Christ. Each went their separate ways on Sunday. The church I was to attend became a big issue between my parents. After much haggling, a compromise was reached. For several years I attended the local Presbyterian Church with friends of my parents who lived nearby. When I became a teenager, my father finally prevailed. For a few years I attended his church, the Church of Christ. I found my father's church rife with intolerance, negativism and self-righteousness. According to his church's teachings, only members of the Church of Christ had a place reserved in heaven.

This was more than I could swallow. This experience turned me against all religions. As an adult, although deeply believing in God, I rejected all organized religion and forged my own direct connection with the Creator. I have become a deist.

Emotional Trauma

There were certain events and relationships occurring in this period of my life that greatly affected the man I was to become. The event I recall most vividly regards my desire for a "Red Ryder BB gun." The classic Christmas movie *A Christmas Story*, although made in the '80s, was set in the late '40s or early '50s, the time of my youth. Like the young boy in the movie, I craved for a Red Ryder BB gun. To have such a gun was my fondest wish, but to no avail. My mother, like the mother in *A Christmas Story*, was afraid I would "shoot my eye out." However, I had a benefactor, my father's younger brother Jim. Jim was about twenty and home on leave from the Marines. To my surprise and delight, he bought me the BB gun I had long cherished. After much discussion between my mother and Uncle Jim, my mother reluctantly agreed to let me keep the BB gun, a decision that would greatly affect my outlook on life.

With the BB gun, I became a real cowboy, a real sharpshooter. At first I was satisfied with sharpening my shooting skills on stationary targets, like tin cans and bottles. This soon became boring. I decided to try my skills on moving objects. I began killing birds, of which there were many which frequented my backyard and those of our neighbors. I proved to be a "crack shot." With each "kill," I would add a notch to the handle of my BB gun, just as I had seen cowboys do in western movies. Then something happened that changed my outlook on death and dying forever.

One afternoon, I spotted a starling in the backyard of the Carey's, a neighbor. Taking aim, I shot and got a direct hit. I was proud of myself as I approached the bird, planning on adding yet another notch to my gun. However, as I approached the bird, I found the bird was still alive and peering at me with sad eyes. I shot the bird from up close to put an end to its misery. I found it remained alive. I shot again and again. The bird refused to die but continued to look at me with haunting eyes. After each shot, I began to sob. By the time life finally left the bird's body, I was lying on the ground weeping uncontrollably and begging the bird's forgiveness. After a while, I composed myself, wiped away my tears, and went into my home. I never related the incident to anyone, not even my parents. However, that day I put the gun in the closet and never picked it up again. I vowed to myself to never kill another living thing. I never have.

Although not one specific event, much of the trauma in my life has been over the vain attempt to win my father's love. In spite of suffering from periodic bouts with depression until I was thirty-nine, I was a relatively high achiever, at least as viewed from afar by other people. In my own mind, I was a failure. The primary focus in my life was to excel so as to win my father's love and approval. With every success, I yearned for my father's praise, which never came. All I felt was a sense of rejection.

Although there are numerous examples of what I perceived as rejection by my father, there was one event from my youth that stands out from the rest. Twelve-year-old boys are probably more sensitive than most, not yet having learned the world is full of rejection and failure and that everyone must deal with an array of personal issues. As a twelve year old, I made the Garrett Drug Company knothole league baseball team. I must admit that, at that time, I was an excellent player, although of the "good field-no hit" variety. Although I often batted a humiliating ninth in the batting order, I excelled in defensive play, defensive play being extremely important in these youthful games.

That year, I was selected for the knothole league all-star team. Before the all-star game was played, there was one regular season game remaining. My father was at that last regular season game. He had attended each regular season game that year but not once had complimented me on my play although others attending the games often had. My father always sat near third base. I played shortstop. Since he had a loud voice that carried, I could overhear many of his comments during the game. In the sixth inning of that last regular season game, my team's left fielder made a spectacular defensive play. Above the cheering, I heard my father say in a loud voice, "It looks like the wrong player made the all-star team." I was devastated. I could not hold back the tears as I kicked the dirt and walked slowly toward second base, hoping the second baseman would not notice my tears. He didn't. No one did.

A Family Tragedy

When I was about nine years old, tragedy struck my family. As you recall, my maternal grandmother and grandfather lived with us. My grandmother became mentally ill. Although at the time the doctors were unable to make a diagnosis, I am sure if she were alive today, she would assuredly be deemed to suffer from depression. This had a two-fold effect on my life. First, it increased the chance that the depression I suffered for so many years had a genetic basis, being inherited from my grandmother. Secondly, watching my grandmother deteriorate before my eyes must have had an ominous effect on my psyche that greatly reinforced the depression I most likely inherited. It was something no child of tender years should have to endure.

At first, my grandmother began to be reclusive, spending most of her time alone, failing to relate to other family members. More and more she would refuse to come out of the bedroom to join in family activities. She would sit in the rocking chair in her bedroom hour after hour. The family realized that this was not "normal"; however, like most people at the time, mental illness was a "taboo" subject and could not possibly affect "our family." It was only after she began incessant mumbling under her breath that my parents and my grandfather realized that she needed help. At first the mumbling was so low as to be unintelligible. Eventually, as her depression progressed, her words were clear, "I can't get no better." Hour after hour, she muttered this same chant. Something had to be done.

My grandfather finally took her to a local psychiatrist. It was the early '50s when nothing was known about depression or the treatment therefore. Antidepressants were in the experimental stage, years away from being utilized effectively. The doctor recommended that she enter in a local psychiatric hospital, often referred to in those days as a "sanitarium" or "asylum." My grandfather knew of nothing else to do.

After she entered the hospital, she seemed to go from bad to worse. Probably knowing nothing else to do, the hospital performed on my grandmother perhaps one of the few treatments known at that time, "shock treatments." The shock treatments did not help. She was eventually transferred to a series of nursing homes until she died in 1967, sixteen years after she first suffered this horrifying disease. Just skin and bones, she often refused to eat and had to be fed intravenously. During these sixteen years, she never stopped her continuous chant, "I can't get no better."

The entire sixteen years that my grandmother was in the nursing homes, each Sunday, all of her children would visit her. I accompanied my parents until I left for college. Of course, my grandfather visited her until his death. Many people assume that because depressed people may mentally withdraw from the world, they have no memory of the past or knowledge of what is happening. My grandmother's actions proved otherwise. While visiting her, her children would often bring up events from their childhood. If they misspoke concerning a certain event, my grandmother would cease her mumbling, speak coherently in a loud voice for a few sentences, often chastising them for their miscue and recounting what actually had happened. She would then resume rubbing her hands and mumbling. She was not incapable of relating to the world. Rather, she had found the world too horrible to endure.

My grandfather was devastated by the love of his life no longer responding to him. She hardly acknowledged his existence. He, himself, went downhill fast. He had always liked his beer, but now he spent many hours at a local tavern trying to escape the torment in his soul. When he was home at night, usually inebriated, he cried incessantly. I often cried along with him. It made me extremely sad to see the grandfather I loved so much suffering so. He visited my grandmother faithfully until his death, but each time returned home sadder than before. A couple of years later, he dropped dead while walking back from the tavern. The doctor diagnosed him of having died from a heart attack. I knew he had died of a broken heart.

3
Puberty

Joining the "Big Boys"

In the fall of 1955 I entered the seventh grade at Central High School in Nashville. Unlike today, when most seventh graders are assigned to Junior High Schools or Middle Schools, Central had grades 7–12. At that time, Central was the only high school for miles around. Most of the students came from poor neighborhoods like mine; however, a few came from "Crieve Hall," a Nashville suburb. Residents of Crieve Hall were not by any means affluent, but the teenagers who resided there were, for the most part, better off economically than most of Central's other students.

There were no black students at Central, just as there were none at any other of the "Lily-white" public schools in Nashville. In 1955, Nashville, like most of the South, was a totally segregated society. The "Separate but Equal" doctrine, left over from antiquated U.S. Supreme Court decisions justifying separate schools for blacks and whites, was the order of the day. When the Supreme Court handed down the decision in "Brown vs. the Board of Education" in 1954, stating that separate schools are inherently unequal, most Southerners realized that it was only a matter of time before their lives would change forever. However, other Southerners, like my parents and other members of my mother's family, were in denial. The chant rang out "Segregation Forever."

With the concept of white supremacy threatened, organized resistance to the "Brown vs. the Board of Education" decision soon flourished. My parents, along with my mother's two brothers and their wives, were easy prey to those preaching racial hatred and fear. They joined a white supremacy organization inappropriately named "Pro Southerners" and were regular attendees at its meetings. In addition, although not members, the aforementioned members of my family, on occasion, paraded with the Ku Klux Klan (KKK). Still a child, I was also "dragged along" on these occasions. Still seared into my memory is the trip to Stone Mountain, Georgia, where we attended a huge "cross burning" along with thousands of people from across the South.

Anyone who has never experienced such an environment cannot begin to understand the effect such an environment can have on a young impressionable child. Every child wants to believe that their parents are good people and are setting an example to guide their path to adulthood. I must confess that for many years I did not see the dark side of my family's values. I carried my family's prejudices with me all through my college years. It was only while serving in the Navy that I got my first glimpse of the "real world," and finally realized what a sick environment I had experienced as a child.

As far as my mental health problems are concerned, nothing changed until about half way through my junior year at Central. Until then, I continued to spend almost all my time outside the classroom "lost in" and somewhat "bewildered by" my own thoughts. It is somewhat ironic that, although when not in school I preferred to be alone, I was fairly popular both with my teachers and the other students. No one, including my family, my teachers or my classmates, realized the dark side of my existence. I was good at putting on a "happy face" and concealing my troubling thoughts.

During my early years at Central, I, experienced obsessive thoughts much of the time, all negative. Disease and danger loomed everywhere. I was surely doomed. I would never reach adulthood. I suffered in silence. However, during this period, I never had a mind-bending full-blown depressive episode. To everyone, I was just a normal, if somewhat shy, young boy. Covering up my disturbing thoughts came easy. Perhaps, the ability to cover up my unhappy thoughts prepared me for future debilitating depressive episodes. Because of my reclusive nature during this period, I was almost completely "cut off" from the teenage world. I did go to Central's basketball and football games, but always alone. Occasionally, a schoolmate, wrongly assuming that I was "normal," would invite me to an outing of one kind or another. I was so self-absorbed that I always declined. Eventually, there were no more invitations.

Sixteen, at Last

During my adolescent years, I had set two goals to achieve when I turned sixteen. Like most of my peers, my primary objective was to obtain a driver's license. No more being carted around by my mother. My other goal was to obtain a part-time job, so that I could have some spending money. Up until I was about fourteen, my father was paid only meager wages, just enough to put clothes on his family's back, food on the table and a roof over our heads. Definitely, luxuries were out. Consequently, my allowance was also paltry.

The day I turned sixteen I took the appropriate test, passed it with flying colors and obtained a necessary rite of passage into adulthood, my driver's license. Next, I became determined to obtain a part-time job. An obvious choice as a potential employer was a local pharmacy, "Garrett Drugs." The owner of the pharmacy had "taken a shine" to me since, when at age twelve, I had been one of the better players on the knothole baseball team he sponsored. Also, it did not hurt that his son had taught the Sunday school class I attended during my years at the neighborhood Presbyterian Church. Shortly after obtaining my driver's license, Garrett Drugs hired me as a "soda jerk," at the grandiose wage of fifty cents an hour. Even in 1959, that was a meager wage. However, since the pharmacy had no shortage of teenage applicants, it was take it or leave it. I took it. During my two years working at the pharmacy, I worked about forty hours each week. This left little time for a social life; however, at the time I was hired in 1959, my prospects for a social life were minimal.

Even though my family was poor, uneducated and considered by most "low class," I had been instilled by my grandfather with values that helped me meet life's challenges. The person I was at sixteen and the person I was later to become was a better person for the lessons learned at my grandfather's knee. I often thank God for his presence in my life during my formative years, although death took him away much too soon. Without the strength and moral guidance he had provided me, I am not sure that I could have survived the period later in life when I was increasingly plagued by overwhelming depression.

Out of My Shell

In the winter of 1960, my junior year at Central, I was dragged, kicking and screaming, from my self-imposed social isolation. I owe it all to Danny, my neighborhood pal from up the street on Morton Avenue for my transformation. Danny was a year ahead of me at Central. I suppose he wanted his legacy at Central to be that he had put together a team of students who would win the election to be 1961's "Student Council." Since he and I had been friends for years, he wanted me to be part of the team he was assembling. Danny's plan was for me to run for "Fire Marshall," a position, perhaps, unique to Central. In most other high schools, a comparable position would be boys' vice-president.

In the winter of my junior year, Danny assembled the persons he was supporting for student council positions along with several others who would work to help our ticket get elected. Steve Hewlett was to run for Student Body President, a good choice since Steve was never at a loss for words. Later in life he was elected to the Tennessee Public Service Commission and was active in Tennessee politics. Annette Siegrist, a quiet but stunning girl, was to run for vice-president. Martha Barrow (Marty), a very popular girl, was to seek the position of Secretary-Treasurer. Betty Shaver, Wanda Scruggs, and Connie Barnett, all of whom would be instrumental in the campaign, were also present at that first meeting and many meetings thereafter.

All four of us were elected and soon became "Big People on Campus." However, for me, the victory was not as important as the fact that, at last, I had become socially active. Being recognized by the other students was a needed shot in the arm for my self-esteem. That same summer, I was introduced into the world of dating. I could tell that my mother was greatly relieved, probably fearing I might be a homosexual. I had fantasized about girls for years, but until I was sixteen, after I had obtained a drivers' license, had secured a job as a "soda jerk" and had achieved recognition by the Central student body, I had never had the wherewithal to actually ask a girl for a date. I finally summoned up the nerve to ask Connie out. To my surprise, she accepted.

That summer, Connie and I began to go out regularly, doing the same lame things our peers were doing. Soon, we were recognized by everyone as a couple. I actually had a girl friend. After beginning to date Connie, much of my social life revolved around Connie and school activities. However, I still spent an inordinate amount of time working at Garrett Drugs. When I got home at 10:30 P.M., I would watch a little TV then go to bed. Other than sharing classes at school, Connie and I saw each other primarily on weekends. Oh yes. My teenage romance was short-lived. We broke up in mid-year of our senior year. She later married a classmate, yet another Bob. They remain happily married to this day. I still feel gratitude to Connie for making me realize, at last, that maybe there were girls out there who would not find me unattractive.

In the latter part of each school year, the "Civitan Award for Good Citizenship" was awarded to a boy in the senior class. Although basically a popularity contest, there was a catch. The principal and the teachers nominated three boys for the award. The award would go to, of these three, the boy with most votes by the senior class. A true popularity contest, of course, would be "wide open," with the senior class being allowed to vote for any member of the class. In truth, some of the more popular students, such as athletes, were not held in high esteem by the principal and teachers. Thus, the choice for winner of the award was narrowed to students who had garnered favor with the school staff. I was among the three members selected by the staff to be considered for the award. My classmates voted me the award. The accolades from my fellow students helped my fledgling self esteem; however, the best news was that during this period in my life, the demons that had ruled my life were, somehow, held at bay.

Preparing for College

My father was highly intelligent and, most likely, could have successfully completed college given the opportunity. When I was in high school, I came across his high school annual. A fellow student had written in the annual, "See you at UT."

My father never made it to UT or any other college. My father's dream had been snuffed out by having the misfortune of being the oldest son in a poverty-stricken family. I suspect that he wanted to live out his fallen dreams through me, his oldest son. For one of the very few times in my life, I felt empathy and sorrow for a man that had been forced to sacrifice his dreams.

While our family was mired in poverty during my adolescence, my father never even mentioned the word "college." Fortunately, when I was about fourteen, my father had gone into business for himself. He was very successful. We would know poverty no more. Suddenly, college became a topic openly discussed in the family. Since my father remembered his extreme disappointment at not being able to attend college, he became determined that I would get that chance. Unfortunately, my grades had suffered, in part, because I had worked six days a week and had little time for studying. The only thing that saved me were my very high scores on the SAT examination. I thought there would be some college out there willing to take a chance on me in spite of my academic record.

In my senior year, I began to consider which college I wished to attend. Although my father's financial status was no longer an issue, my father did not wish to pay the exorbitant tuition at private schools. He preferred that I go to a state school. That was fine with me. My father's preference was that for two years I go to a state school thirty miles from Nashville, then go to the University of Tennessee (UT) in Knoxville my final two years. I wanted to spend my entire college years at one place. My father finally relented and agreed I could attend UT in the fall if they would accept me. I applied the next day and was quickly accepted.

My primary reason for wanting to attend UT was that it was about the right distance from home. At 200 miles from Nashville, it was close enough that I could come home when necessary, yet far enough away that I would not be under the watchful eye of my parents. At last, I could escape the unhappiness of my dysfunctional family and make my own way in the world. I would be free to forge a new life for myself and seek my own dreams. At last, I would have a better life. But life does not always go as planned. Little did I know that a little over a year later my world would come crashing down.

4
Coming of Age

Adapting to College Life

In late August 1961, I was off to the University of Tennessee (UT). I loaded all my "stuff" in the family station wagon. My mother drove me to Knoxville to enter me into the university. My father, as usual, was too preoccupied to accompany us.

My mother confessed years later the anxiety that she experienced at seeing her "baby boy" leave the nest. I soon got settled in my dorm room in New Melrose Hall. My mother then left me with a tearful farewell. After driving about seventy miles toward our home in Nashville, crying all the way, my mother turned the car around and drove back to Knoxville to retrieve her son and take him home with her. When my mother arrived at the entrance to my dorm, after driving the seventy miles, she suddenly realized how foolhardy her mission was. After contemplating for a few minutes what action she should take, she at last realized the finality of my leaving home and once again headed back to Nashville, this time completing the trip. I was so excited at starting a new adventure that I was clueless about how hard it is for a mother to let go.

I had practically no social life my freshman year, somewhat reverting to the shy, introverted guy I had once been. I was soon brought back down to earth. I was no longer a "big man on campus" as I had been my senior year at Central. I was now simply a little fish in a big pond.

My lack of social contact with girls that first year at UT was essentially my own fault. Several girls in my classes gave me encouraging signs; however, I was either too socially inept or too foolish to follow up on their overtures. That first year I went home often, in fact, being somewhat homesick. That changed as I progressed through college. My last couple of years at UT, I went home only at Christmas and for a brief visit prior to working out of state during the summer. I must admit that during that first year at UT, just about the most excitement I had was rushing to the mailbox every day to see if anyone had written me. Usually I was disappointed. The only mail I received was from my mother and from Ann, a sophomore at Saint Bernard's Academy in Nashville, whom I had dated the previous summer. I was grateful for each letter. In spite of my lonely existence that freshman year, I had no signs of clinical depression. I was just a lonely young man.

I must confess that during my freshman year I had all the earmarks of being a typical nerd. I did little else except study. I barely missed making the Dean's List the first quarter but made it the second and third quarter. However, something did happen in the spring quarter that would greatly influence not only my college life but my own self-image as well. Wayne Harris, a Central graduate and a year ahead of me at UT, suddenly appeared in my life. In high school, I had only known him casually.

Early that spring, out of the blue, Wayne called me and asked me to join him in a round of golf. I jumped at the chance to escape an otherwise boring existence. That spring we played golf several times at a course in Maryville, a few miles from Knoxville. Wayne had wheels, a classic 1957 Chevy, which made our golf outings in Maryville possible. I soon learned that Wayne had a hidden agenda in asking me to play golf. It seems Wayne had partied a bit too much his first two years at UT and was in academic trouble. Having learned that I was a "book worm," he asked me if, during the following fall quarter, I would like to share an off campus apartment with himself and John McKenzie, another Nashville native. Wayne had also ascertained that John had made good grades during his two years at UT. I was elated, assuring him that I was "all in" for the arrangement. Little did I know what the next year would have in store for me, both socially and psychologically.

"Meltdown"

In the summer between my freshman and sophomore years at UT, I worked in my father's print shop as I had done the previous summer after finishing high school. Making substantially more than the fifty cents per hour that I had made during high school while working as a soda jerk, I had saved a considerable bankroll. During my college years, a major portion of my earnings went toward meeting my college expenses. However, in the summer of 1962, I was adamant about using a small portion of my earnings to purchase a used car to take back to UT in the fall. I was not unrealistic. Any old "jalopy" would do. At first, my father was resolute that my buying a car was out of the question. I imagine he thought that, with wheels, I would "go wild" and my grades would suffer.

Fortunately, my uncle, my mother's oldest brother, intervened in my behalf. On most subjects except race he was both a wise and reasonable man. He convinced my father that since I had made the Dean's List my first year at UT and, in my youth, had never given my father the slightest problem, my father should "cut me some slack" and let me have a car. My father, at last, relented. I could have a car. I purchased my "dream car" from a neighbor. It was a solid black 1956 Chevy. Although the car was six years old at the time I bought it, for the following six years I drove that car all over the country during my college years and my years in the Navy.

In the fall of 1962, life could not have been any better. I was an honors student, with wheels, off to experience my sophomore year in college and to share an off-campus apartment with two other students. Little did I know that my world would soon come crashing down.

When I arrived in Knoxville, I was greeted by Wayne and, for the first time, met John, my other roommate. John was a Catholic who had graduated from Father Ryan High School in Nashville. Like Wayne, he was a year ahead of me in school. A chemistry major, John had made good grades his two years at UT. A good academic record was the criteria Wayne had used in choosing John and me to be his roommates. Nevertheless, John was a also "free spirit," prone to do the unexpected. An example of John's eccentricity was his purchase, for $50, of a "clunker" to drive from Nashville to Knoxville, with all his "stuff." The windows on the car would not roll up. John drove the 200 miles in a driving rainstorm, all the way with rain flying in his face. After arriving in Knoxville, he abandoned this "piece of crap." That's John.

After settling in our apartment, I soon met three students who lived on the first floor of our apartment building, with whom Wayne, John and I soon became fast friends. Danny, Henry and Fred were transfer students from Tusculum College. All three were from New Jersey. They had headed south to obtain an education because Southern colleges were much cheaper, even after paying out-of-state tuition, than colleges in the northeast. Unfortunately, they were uncomfortable at Tusculum College, a strict church-related college. Particularly perplexing to them were the strict rules regarding interaction between the sexes. They would soon find the open-minded atmosphere at UT more to their liking. In addition to Danny, Henry and Fred, I cultivated many other friendships that fall, including Felder and Emory. I have found that my college friends would be friends for life.

Wayne had greatly overestimated the influence John and I would have on his lifestyle. I suppose he had anticipated that, rooming with two "bookworms," our apartment would become a glorified study hall. Much to his dismay (or maybe to his delight), our apartment, instead, soon became "Party Central." Of course, by today's standards, our parties were probably tame. However, partying, not studying became the password for that quarter.

Fall quarter, 1962, was a joyous time. However, all good things have to end. Little did I know when I first arrived at UT that, before the quarter was over, I would begin to encounter my first truly "depressive episode." Depressive episodes, unfortunately, would follow me for the next twenty years. About two or three weeks before December exams, I realized a change was coming over me. Although I had had a troubled soul in my youth, somehow, this was different. At nineteen, I had no knowledge of depression, even though if I had thought about it, I would have remembered those sixteen debilitating years my maternal grandmother had suffered years before.

As exams approached that fall, I sank deeper and deeper into what was to become a full-blown depressive episode. Neither Wayne, John nor my other friends suspected the emotional trauma that I was going through. Somehow, I made it through the exams although I felt that the exams had been a disaster for me. During each exam, my ability to concentrate on the subject at hand was more or less "shot." Random thoughts, having nothing to do with the exams, permeated my thinking. After I finished the exams, I dreaded receiving my grades while home during Christmas vacation. What if I failed them all? What would my parents think? What would happen to me?

After the term was over, I said farewell to Wayne and John, wondering if I would ever see them again. I cried most of the way from Knoxville to Nashville. Crying, while alone, had become a habit. I wondered how I could possibly get through Christmas, with my family full of cheer while I was filled with gloom and horrible thoughts. However, when I arrived home, I put on my "happy face." My family was oblivious to my fragile psyche.

Somehow, I made it through Christmas. Even though my pessimistic nature had feared the worst, when my grades arrived, I found I had done fairly well and remained in good standing with the university. I was surprised that I had not flunked out. But what was I to do now? My family was so proud of me. Dare I tell my parents that I wanted to drop out of school? In my mind, that was not an option. When the time came to return to school, with much fear and trepidation, I kissed my mother good-bye and set out for Knoxville. As had become a habit, I cried most of the way.

In Knoxville, Wayne, John and my other friends all celebrated. No one had flunked out. We were all back for winter quarter. Had anyone had any doubts that we would all return? I soon registered for the subjects I had chosen, but neither my heart nor mind was in it. After going to the first class in each of my subjects, I realized that I could not remember one thing from any of the classes. The days of faking my way through life were over. I had no choice but to drop out of school and face the consequences. Everyone, including my family, would just have to think of me as they wished. It was on a Sunday night that I made the final decision to drop out, even though I knew not what the future held for me.

Even in my depressed state, there was orderliness in my madness. Sunday night, I made plans of how to face the situation. I did not tell Wayne and John immediately of my decision even though it would affect them greatly. Monday morning, I went to UT officials and informed them of my decision to drop out. They reviewed my academic record and appeared astounded. Ashamed of my real reason for dropping out, I gave them a song and dance about having girlfriend troubles in Nashville that I needed to address before continuing my education. I assured them that I would return for the spring quarter. Of course, in my own mind, I never expected to see UT again. They bought my story and sent me on my way saying that I would be welcome back in the spring. To me, spring was an eternity away.

That same morning, after I returned from seeing the UT officials, I wrote my parents, telling them of my decision to drop out of school. Writing that letter was the hardest thing I had ever done. I could not help but weep while writing the letter, for I knew that I was spoiling all of their hopes and dreams for me. Fortunately, Wayne and John were in classes and were not present to witness my emotional freefall. In my heart, I knew that dropping out of school seemed like an irrational thing to do. But with my mind in turmoil, what else could I do?

That afternoon, I went to the post office and mailed the letter, knowing that it would arrive at my parents' home Wednesday afternoon. I knew that I must not arrive home before the letter. I wanted to give them a few hours to adjust to the situation before I made an appearance. On Tuesday, I pretended to go to classes. Instead, I went to Concord Park. In winter it is a secluded location. I stayed there for hours dwelling on what a mess that I was making of my life. I cried a lot. Crying seemed to come easy those days.

On Wednesday morning, I told Wayne and John of my decision. Shocked understates their reaction. I did not explain to them my reason for dropping out, only that it was something I had to do. They could not understand. Could anybody? Because money meant nothing to me at that point, I gave them my share of the February and March rent and assured them that I would return in the spring, not believing a word that I said.

After my farewells with Wayne and John, I started out for Nashville. Upon nearing my home in Nashville, I, once again, tried to put on my "game face." I knew it would not work this time. As expected, even with a few hours to "get over" the news, it was obvious that my mother and father were devastated. I can't remember what was said. I only knew the charade was over. After a few minutes, I went up to my bedroom and went to sleep. I slept peacefully that night. I had finally given up. I did not have to fake it anymore.

I was seeking a sanctuary where I would be safe and free from the heartaches of the world. For several days, I got out of bed only to eat and use the bathroom. I would never have gotten out of that bed of my own volition. However, my father concluded that I was just lazy or a slacker. He demanded that beginning the next day, I was to accompany him to the print shop and help him with his work. As usual, I complied. Did I really have a choice?

For a few weeks, I dutifully accompanied him and worked with him in the print shop. Fortunately, my work was on the opposite end of the print shop from where my father ran the printing machine. He rarely came over to where I was. When he did, I wiped away my tears and pretended nothing was wrong. At night, I went to bed soon after dinner. I wondered how long that I could go on like this.

One morning in late February, when my life appeared as if it would forever lie in ruins, I woke up and thought I envisioned a glimpse of hope. For the following two weeks, each day I found that I was, incrementally, in better spirits than the day before. Each day was a step forward. Was it possible that I could survive this ordeal? Finally, one Sunday afternoon, in mid-March, I went to the far corner of our backyard and for hours contemplated my future. Could I make it if I went back to UT or was I just experiencing false hope? What if I tried and failed? On the other hand, what kind of life did I face if I did not try? What future was there for me here?

The following day I informed my father that I wanted to go back to school. My father appeared glad that I had decided to return to UT, although he never expressed his feelings or his emotions. That afternoon, I called UT and asked to be admitted for the spring quarter. They stated that they would welcome me back with open arms. My next call was to Wayne and John. They seemed thrilled that I was returning.

I realized that I was not yet out of the woods. The fear of having another depressive episode haunted me continuously from that day forth. Still, I somehow felt that I could make it. I now realize that the experience that fall and winter may have helped me in the future when I encountered even more devastating episodes of depression. I suppose that once you have seen the bottom, it inspires you to never give up no matter how hopeless life might appear. At any rate, I was off to UT once more.

Finishing College

After I returned for spring quarter, things had not changed much from the "goings on" fall quarter. Only this time, I more fully appreciated college life, having seen the dark side of life. For the time being, I felt that I had experienced the worst life had to offer and had, somehow, "faced it down." Little did I know that, in the not too distant future, I would find that my nightmare in the winter of 1963 would be repeated more than once. I did not realize that I had only seen the tip of the iceberg.

From the time I experienced my "meltdown" in the winter of 1963 until I graduated from UT in December 1965, I experienced only fleeting bouts of depression. These episodes were short-lived, usually lasting, at most, a couple of weeks. They were also not so severe as to seriously impair my ability to "think" or function. I soon learned that these "mini-episodes" would pass if only I would "tough it out." I began to realize that these pitfalls were probably inevitable, something I would just have to learn to live with, maybe, for the rest of my life.

Throughout my years at UT, our "crowd" played revolving roommates. We saw so much of each other it mattered not who roomed with whom. In the fall of 1963, while I was rooming with Felder (Sonny), an event occurred that changed the perspective of life not only for my friends and me but for a whole generation.

I was taking a nap in my bedroom a little after noon one November day. A radio was on in our kitchen but was barely audible in our bedroom. As I was drifting in and out, I heard what seemed to be extreme excitement from the voice on the radio. Curious, I rushed into the kitchen. The president that my generation almost universally worshipped, John F. Kennedy, had been assassinated. The pain of the assassination has probably lingered, to this day, somewhere in the back of all our minds. November 22, 1963 was the end of innocence and the onset of cynicism for a whole generation of disillusioned young Americans.

I cannot write about my college life without touching on my relationships, or lack thereof, with the opposite sex. In truth, with one exception, there was nothing even approaching a relationship with a girl or woman during my four years at UT. When not partying with my friends, I spent much of my time trying to be a scholastic high achiever, hoping, in vain, that being an honor student would gain my father's love. Most dates that I had were inconsequential.

The exception was Marilyn, a brilliant girl from upper east Tennessee that I met at the university book store in early September 1963. She had just reported for her freshman year at UT. There was nothing approaching love in our relationship.

Throughout the years during which we knew each other while at UT, we would see each other for awhile, then not date for awhile, and then, ultimately, reconnect. While we were apart, I imagine her "dance card" was full. Marilyn and I genuinely liked each other, had great fun when together, and had an abiding respect for one another. Even today, I believe that she is only one of a handful of people that I have known in my life who truly understood my depth and intensity. I regret that I did not have the wherewithal to pursue the relationship further.

I have not related how I spent my summers during my college years. Prior to 1964, in the summer, I worked in Nashville at my father's print shop, saving money to partially pay for my college expenses. In the summers of 1964 and 1965, I took a different tack, working in an auditor training program for a large national corporation.

The summer of 1964, I worked in Jacksonville, Florida, at one of my employer's many sites throughout the country. In truth, although a sun worshipper who enjoyed the beach or a pool, the summer was quite uneventful. I had only a handful of dates the entire summer, none of which amounted to anything. Even though I lived in an apartment complex known as "sin city," as far as my experience that summer was concerned, it was a misnomer. The summer of 1964 was very forgettable, but a blip on the radar screen of my life.

After finishing my next to last quarter at UT in the spring of 1965, I began, for the first time to seriously consider my future. It would seem that the logical thing to do would be to go to school during the summer quarter at UT and graduate in August. But there was one problem, Vietnam. There was no doubt that I would be drafted into the military soon after graduation. Like so many others of my generation, I chose to be in denial and put off such an eventuality. The corporation that I had worked for in 1964 in Jacksonville offered me the opportunity to work at their regional office in Charlotte, North Carolina, the summer of 1965. Like a drowning man desperate for rescue, I accepted their offer.

Common sense should have told me that I was simply putting off the inevitable. However, hope springs eternal in desperate people. I kept clinging to an irrational thought, maybe, by December when I was to graduate, the war would be over. At any rate, life waits for no man.

At the completion of spring quarter, I set out for Charlotte, not knowing that the events that transpired that summer would greatly affect my life. Thanks to Roger, a neighbor of mine at 500 Beechway Circle, where I settled in, I had quite a few dates that summer. Roger had an "in" at a nearby school for nursing. However, my future had a dark cloud hanging over it thanks to the war in Vietnam. I wanted no serious relationship.

I had no sooner arrived in Charlotte when I met Miranda (Randy) at the apartment complex pool. Both being sun worshippers, we spent many hours at the pool on Saturdays and Sundays. Even though I was very much attracted to Randy, I was intimidated by her. She was a couple of years older and had recently undergone a painful divorce. My natural shyness and her understandable mistrust of men made it seem highly unlikely that we would ever "hit it off." As the summer wore on, Randy and I became fast friends, far from the relationship that I desired. We spoke very openly to each other, telling each other things about ourselves that we had probably confided to very few people. Yet, I never got up the nerve to ask Randy out. Late that summer, I left Charlotte to return to UT. I never expected to see Randy again.

There is one footnote to my life that I must mention. After leaving Charlotte and before reaching Knoxville, I made a side trip of much importance to me. I drove straight from Charlotte to Jackson, Tennessee, to be the best man in Wayne's marriage to the love of his life, Nan. Yes, lady's man Wayne, my old roommate and best friend, had finally been corralled. Nan was and is a wonderful person. He could not have done better. Years later, Wayne and Nan and I reconnected at one of our college reunions. Wayne and Nan and my wife and I became the closest of friends. We had several vacations together, mostly to various Caribbean islands.

After I returned to UT in the fall of 1965, I had no social life to speak of that quarter. The only girl that I would have liked to have seen, Marilyn, had graduated the previous summer. I was not interested in seeking dates. Being there for such a short time, what was the point? I was obsessed with one thought, Vietnam.

In September, I learned from my draft board that I would probably be drafted the first month after graduation in December. I panicked. What would I do? Being a patriotic American, running off to Canada to live was not an option, although many others chose that alternative. However, the thought of being a foot soldier in Vietnam sent cold chills down my spine. There must be some way out of this dilemma.

In spite of the fact that I had a history of car sickness and sea sickness, desperate, I went to the Navy recruiting station and sought entrance in the Navy Officer Training Program. At first the Navy recruiter was skeptical due to my eyesight; however, he gave me a ray of hope. There was one branch of the Navy that did not require officers to have perfect vision, the Supply Corps. He was, however, discouraging, informing me that due to the draft, many college graduates were seeking entry into Navy Officer Training School (OCS). Nevertheless, I took the entrance exam and, even though not overly religious, prayed. I must admit that I omitted telling the recruiter of my "meltdown" in the winter of 1963 or my other bouts with depression. I knew that would automatically have caused me to be rejected. Besides, that was all behind me, wasn't it?

Rejoice! I was accepted! However, there was one hitch. The next opening for OCS was in mid-April 1966. Unfortunately, I would most likely be drafted long before April. The

Navy gave me a way out of my dilemma. I took the oath of office. The Navy immediately put me in the Naval Reserve, where I could not be drafted.

After taking the oath, I felt like I had just dodged a big bullet. At last, I was worry free. Ignorance is bliss. It did not occur to me that OCS might be a "grinding ordeal" that would test my character, intestinal fortitude and mental stability. For the time being, my primary concern was what I would do between graduation and entering OCS in April. My concern soon disappeared.

At the beginning of the fall quarter, with an unusual display of optimism, I had signed up for interviews with several prospective employers. Later I cancelled most of the interviews, all but one. I thought that, in spite of my draft status, I should interview this particular national CPA firm. Perhaps, I would have a better chance with them after completing my military commitment.

Even though the CPA firm recruiters were from their Chattanooga office, when they found that I had worked in Charlotte the previous summer, they indicated that there were openings in the Charlotte office for "green recruits." Actually, my situation, leaving in mid-April for the Navy, gave me a "leg up" when I subsequently interviewed in the Charlotte office, since January through April was their "busy season." It would also be a "trial run" for subsequent employment after my commitment to the Navy was over.

I graduated from UT with honors on the twentieth of December 1965. After a few days at home for Christmas, on Wednesday, December 29, I set out for Charlotte. Due to the numerous "inventory observations" to be held by the firm the last day of the year, my first day of work was to be December 31. Life seemed good. Little did I know that in the not too distant future, I would experience both an enormous high and a tremendous low.

At Last, Love

Late at night, Wednesday December 29, I arrived in Charlotte in my trusty '56 Chevy carrying all my earthly belongings. I stayed at a motel that night. The next morning, I started on my quest to find a place to live for the next three and one-half months. As can be expected of an inexperienced young man, I had not planned ahead. I just assumed that I could get an apartment on Beechway Circle where I had lived the previous summer. The owner informed me there were no vacancies.

I almost panicked. I had to find a place and move in that very day. I was to report for work with the CPA firm the following morning. The owner did give me a few suggestions on possibly vacant apartments. I immediately followed up on his leads. By late that afternoon, I had moved into an older apartment on the opposite side of town from Beechway Circle. It was not as nice as the apartments on Beechway Circle but it was adequate for my needs. By that night, I had settled in.

The next morning, Friday, New Year's Eve, I reported for work. Since I had met quite a few of the employees on my interview the previous fall, introductions were, in most cases, unnecessary. I was told not to worry about my inexperience. The senior on my first job, nicknamed "Fireball" after a famous NASCAR driver, was one of their top senior auditors and would guide me in carrying out my audit work. I left that day, confident I would fit in nicely with this firm.

As soon as I left the office that afternoon, I stopped by my apartment and changed into something casual. I set out for Beechway Circle, my old "stomping grounds," hoping Roger, would still live there. Not only was he home, he was planning a spontaneous New Year's Eve "bash." Roger was busy rounding up as many people as he could. Eagerly, I volunteered to go see Randy, with whom I was "smitten" the previous summer, to find out if she was available and interested in the party.

Happily, Randy was home. She seemed happy to see me. She was also interested in going to Roger's party. Actually, when I first arrived, she confessed she had been in a foul mood and was down on men. It seems that she had received three last-minute invitations that afternoon for New Year's Eve parties from male friends. Not wanting to be any man's "last minute desperation date," she had declined and was resigned to spending New Year's Eve alone. Since I had arrived in Charlotte only two days before, she did not hold the late invitation against me.

Randy and I went to Roger's party together. While most of the people intermingled, we spent the whole night together, dancing, catching up on each other's lives, and just generally enjoying each other's company. After the obligatory kiss bringing in the New Year, we left the party. I walked her to her apartment. Surprisingly, after we kissed goodnight, she asked me if I wanted to come over the next day and watch the New Year's Day football bowl games. Remembering that only the previous summer she had told me that she hated football, I was elated. I knew that I was "in."

In the following three months prior to my leaving for Naval OCS, Randy and I spent almost every day together. We ate dinner in local restaurants and attended concerts, movies and hockey games. But most of all, we just enjoyed being together. It was not long before I decided that, assuredly, Randy was the love of my life. I knew she felt the same way.

Unfortunately, all good things must come to an end. About the first of April, two weeks before I was to leave, I realized it was "decision time." What was I to do? Should I ask Randy to marry me now or, at the latest, in August after I completed OCS? I was confident that if I proposed she would accept. I could see it in her eyes even though she was too proud to bring up the subject of marriage. However, I knew that during my three years in the Navy, I would likely be assigned to ships going all over the world. Would marrying her now or in August be a wise decision?

Being only twenty-two, I was young and naïve in the ways of the world and in particular the ways of love. Or perhaps I was just getting "cold feet." Surely, in three years, after I completed my commitment to the Navy, both of us still being young, we would still be in love and could marry at that time. We would have a lifetime to be together.

In mid-April, Randy and I had a tearful good-bye. We pledged our undying love and promised to write often. Was leaving her a mistake? I would have a lifetime to decide. As I set out for a brief stay in Nashville before reporting to OCS, I should have remembered the words that, as a child, I once heard my mother tell one of her friends:

Absence makes the heart grow fonder,
for somebody else.

5
Military Service

Naval Officer Candidate School

To get to Newport, Rhode Island, from Nashville, I had to fly to Providence, then take a bus to Newport. I left on a Thursday in mid-April. The bus to Newport from Providence was filled, almost exclusively, with others bound for Navy Officer Candidate School (OCS). There was much merriment. You would have thought that we were heading to a beach for spring break rather than to a site where, for eighteen weeks, we would face the severest challenge of our young lives.

After the bus arrived in Newport, almost everyone headed for the lounge at the Viking Motel, which was to become a "hangout" for a lot of officer candidates while on liberty that summer. Most of us got "smashed," facing a hangover the following morning when we were to report for the OCS program.

As soon as we arrived at the Naval Station Friday morning, we were assigned to sixteen-man companies. I was assigned to Charlie Company, forever being known that summer as a member of Charlie 6-13. Some of the other members of Charlie Company were those I had met on the bus from Providence. Others were not. We immediately developed a "one for all, all for one" mentality. Each member's duty was to help other members of Charlie Company somehow survive. That summer, when someone was having trouble academically or in any other way, everyone helped pull them through.

The first weekend was a "weekend from hell." There was the obligatory shaving of heads, issuing of uniforms, etc. Then the "fun" began. Our job was to make spotless, from stem to stern, Nimitz Hall, our home away from home during much of our stay in Newport. I wondered, *What have I gotten myself into*? One of my jobs was to clean the grating between floor tiles with a toothbrush, a task which lasted long into the night. None of us got much sleep that weekend.

Almost every member of the April class was in OCS for one reason, to avoid the draft. Academically, it was an elite class. In Charlie Company alone, we had several members with degrees from prestigious universities. One was a graduate of Yale, another Harvard. Most had never considered serving in the military until the draft board reared its ugly head. Some had been "anti-war activists." We were soon dubbed by some hardcore skeptical navy men as "Hippies in uniform."

If one wants to get an accurate portrayal of life as a navy officer candidate, one should see the 1982 movie *An Officer and a Gentleman* with Richard Gere and Debra Winger. Of course, the movie was dramatized for effect; nevertheless, I always laughingly tell friends that I could relate well to that movie in all respects except two: (1) We trained for duty on surface ships, not airplanes and (2) During my time in Newport, I never met a woman like Debra Winger.

I almost panicked during the first few days in Newport. I realized that I was sinking into a depressive episode. I prayed it would only be minor and last a couple of weeks like the "mini episodes" that I had endured several times while in college. But what if it was a "meltdown" like in 1963? I only knew that I had to somehow get through each day. I had no other options.

When *An Officer and a Gentleman* was made, the movie revealed that in 1982, an officer candidate could just quit and return home. The movie called it DOR (Drop on Request). That was true in 1982 but not in 1966. In 1966, if one washed out, quit the program or left the program for any reason other than family hardship or medical problems, the officer candidate went straight to the fleet as a Seaman Recruit, the lowest enlisted rank in the Navy. A great incentive to "hang in there."

I slept little the first three weeks. To add insult to injury, officer candidates were confined to base the first three weeks. I lay awake well into the night, dreading "reveille." We would start the day off with fifteen minutes of calisthenics in the hallway. This would begin the day where we would go "full blast," either in physical exercises or academic training in naval subjects. How could I make it through another day? Somehow I managed. Thank God, the depressive episode was only a "minor" one and lasted only a couple of weeks. When we got liberty after the first three weeks, I had a ray of hope that somehow I could survive the program.

Being in the Navy, the ability to swim was essential. Our class had to go through extensive training in the art of swimming. Early on, I performed the essential requirements to get my commission as an officer. That was not an issue. However, the class, each day, had extensive training in different strokes. A classmate, Mike and I could not keep up with the class. We were assigned to "stupid swim," a role as humiliating as the name implies.

"Stupid Swim" was held during the only hour of the day that the rest of our classmates were given a break and allowed to do as they pleased. It was a punishment for not being able to keep up with the class. At first, Mike and I worked hard to improve our swimming skills. We soon realized it was hopeless. We would be in "stupid swim" for the remainder of our stay in Newport. But every cloud has its silver lining. A couple of weeks later, our company was so horrible at marching in "Pass in Review" before liberty on Saturday that every other member of our company, for weeks, had to practice marching in the broiling summer sun while Mike and I "lolly-gagged" around the pool. Although our classmates made fun of Mike and me for being so inept at swimming, we got the last laugh.

While at OCS, Randy and I exchanged letters faithfully. Without those letters, I might have "tossed in the towel." I could not wait to see her again. Her letters gave me the strength to endure. Being a young man with raging hormones, there were many times when I questioned my commitment to be true to Randy. Temptation abounded!

Each weekend, the "Fall River Queens," as we called them, came down from Fall River, Massachusetts, for a Navy sponsored dance at the Officers' Club. The expectations of the single young women from Fall River and the officer candidates were quite different. Most of the young women were looking for husbands. The officer candidates just wanted to get laid. Although one member of Charlie Company did later marry one of these young women, generally speaking, the expectations of the officer candidates were often fulfilled, while the young women usually went back to Fall River waiting for the next weekend.

The officer candidates got liberty from around noon, Saturday until 6:00 P.M. Sunday after the first three weeks during which we were confined to quarters. Those of us not chasing "Fall River Queens" often spent much of our weekends at the Viking Motel lounge getting drunk. A popular song of the era by the pop group, "The Animals" reverberated throughout the lounge as the officer candidates, feeling no pain, sang over and over again "We've Got to Get Out of This Place." Somehow, singing that song made us all feel better, at least until we reported back to OCS Sunday at 6:00 P.M.

Although I was faithful to Randy, I did have a couple of casual dates of no consequence. There is one incident that I feel compelled to relate although it more or less "puts me in my place." One July Sunday, in Newport, Jim Seaborg, a classmate, and I met two young women on Newport Beach. When we met these two young women, it was 2:00 P.M. We were due back at our barracks at 6:00 P.M. Therefore, we were merely off on a lark, with no expectations. Nevertheless, we convinced these young women to go riding up and down the Newport Beach area in Jim's convertible. Just as we were having a great time, the woman in the back seat with me turned to me and said in a loud voice, "You sound just like Gomer Pyle!" The other three got a good belly laugh at my expense. Being sensitive to my "redneck" persona and accent, I did not think it was funny.

Of the sixteen original members of Charlie Company, fourteen got their commissions as naval officers. Of the two who did not graduate with the rest of us, one received a hardship discharge because of family illness. The loss of our other comrade both shocked and dismayed us. After a few weeks, one of our number "washed out" due to academic deficiencies. Callously, after he was demoted to Seaman Recruit, the Navy did not ship him out to a new duty station, but relegated him to picking up trash around our compound. Each day, as we went about our daily routine, we saw him and all his humiliation. To the Navy, it was just a warning to the rest of us what could happen if we did not "shape up." It was effective.

On August 19, 1966, the fourteen remaining members of Charlie Company took our oath of office and became Ensigns in the U.S. Navy. There was elation all around. As is customary, the drill instructor who guided us through the eighteen-week ordeal was the first to salute us. In return, each new Ensign handed him a silver dollar. We had made it. After graduation, all the members of Charlie Company were off to parts unknown, most never to meet again. But wherever each of us may be, I know each of us has a special place in their hearts for their comrades who shared this experience. I am sorry to report that one member of Charlie Company died in a boating accident shortly after graduation. It was a lesson often lost on most young people, "Life is fragile and temporary."

The navy had accomplished, in me, what they had set out to do. They had broken me down and rebuilt me in the image that they desired. I was prouder of that Ensign stripe than anything I had accomplished in the past. Maybe now my father would be proud of me and give me his unconditional love. I wore my uniform on the flight home. My family was at the airport to greet me. My mother, with tears in her eyes, caressed me. My father stood nearby, not saying a word. That day, I gave up trying to win his love. From that day forward, I would be my own man.

Naval Supply Corps School

After a brief visit home, I was off to the U.S. Naval Supply Corps School in Athens, Georgia. There I hooked up with four other members of Charlie Company who were also assigned to the Supply Corps School. Athens would have been only a typical small southern town except that it was home to the University of Georgia. Athens, far from the ocean, would seem like an unlikely location for a large naval facility. Athens was chosen as the home of the Navy Supply Corps School due to the enormous influence of the Georgia delegation in the U.S. Congress.

After the trauma of OCS, the Navy Supply Corps School seemed like a paradise. The six months spent there were more like a vacation. Of course, since those attending the school were all commissioned officers, there was no harassment by the school staff as there had been in Newport. The atmosphere surrounding the school was "laid back," much like the city of Athens itself. One "perk" for those attending the supply school was, being a federal facility, the officers' club had the only legal alcohol within a fifty- or sixty-mile radius of Athens. The officers' club was nicely done and proved a magnet for University of Georgia coeds. Some of the university's staff, including the head football coach, also frequented the officers' club.

As for my state of mind while in Athens, for the most part I was depression free. I felt that the "meltdown" in the winter of 1963 while I was at UT had been but an aberration. Surely, it was a one-time occurrence. As for Randy, I could not wait to see her. At the first opportunity, on a Friday, I set out for Charlotte to spend the weekend.

I touched base with Randy the week before I was to go. During that conversation, I got my first hint that something had changed. Randy had moved across town from Beechway Circle and had acquired a roommate. She informed me that because of her sharing an apartment, it would not be best for me to plan on staying with her. Disappointed, I called one of my friends still living on Beechway Circle and asked if I could "crash" for the weekend. He was happy to have me stay with him.

I was stunned when I visited Randy that weekend. It was obvious that on her part the intensity of the relationship had vanished. I left Charlotte that weekend with much upon which to reflect. Just where did I stand with Randy, who I still thought of as the love of my life? Had she found someone else? Had she simply found that she no longer felt as I did? Either way, it gave me a sick feeling in the pit of my stomach.

Academically, the supply school was tough; however, after OCS, it seemed like a "piece of cake." There was a great deal of competition among the members of the class to achieve academic excellence. It was a matter of pride. Periodically, the school would release the class ranking of each student. Just as at OCS, I was in the middle of the pack. The "Hotshot" from UT had more than met his match.

As for my relationship with Randy, I made two more trips to Charlotte while stationed at Athens to try and rekindle the flame of love that I feared might have been extinguished. It was no use. Things were just not the same. Most likely, they never would be. As graduation approached, I realized that I could not spend the next three years "eating my heart out" over a love that seemed doomed. I decided that henceforth I would be open to meeting women and "let the chips fall where they may." But I realized that I owed Randy a lot. One never completely gets over their first love. For the first time in my life I had known the feeling of loving and being loved in return.

In March 1967, our class faced graduation. Unlike OCS, there were no casualties. Nobody was booted out. As I mentioned before, the class was ranked academically. The class ranking was used to determine each officer's assigned duty station. Even the last person in the class was sure of being assigned somewhere. When the class assembled in March, each officer was told the duty station to which he was assigned. Disappointed, my fate was held in "limbo." I was assigned to the COMCRUDESPAC "pool" in San Diego. I would have to wait for it to be ultimately determined where I would spend a large part of the next three years.

The "pool" consists of a couple of officers on each coast who stood ready to report for duty at a moment's notice to replace someone who was being relieved of their duties. Relieving a supply officer most likely would be for health reasons, but could be for any one of a number of reasons, including incompetence. An officer assigned to the pool could be in the pool from five minutes to the maximum of about two months. After the officer was assigned a duty station, a recent graduate of the supply school would take their place in the pool.

After graduation, I quickly left for Nashville for two or three weeks at home. In spite of not knowing my ultimate assignment, I felt like I had the "world by the tail." Two and a half years of adventure lie ahead. Little did I know that in about two months I would have a "meltdown" far worse than that experienced in the winter of 1963. God is benevolent in not allowing man to see into the future.

Lost Summer

After about three weeks at home, I set out for San Diego. It was late April when I reported to the COMCRUDESPAC pool in San Diego. The office where I was to work was located on the huge Naval Base at San Diego. I settled in at the Bachelor Officers' Quarters (BOQ) which, fortunately, was only a short walk to the office where I was to spend my time awaiting assignment.

I spent several weeks in the pool awaiting orders. During those weeks, there were no emergencies in the ships under COMCRUDESPAC command. While awaiting orders, I mostly participated in "make work" projects of little consequence or studied manuals which bored me to tears. After work each day, things got considerably brighter. I met several other junior officers at the BOQ with which I soon began to "hang out." Being a Navy city, there were a number of bars within a short distance of the BOQ, where we could frequently be found. However, the highlight of the week was Friday night when several of us regularly attended a dance at, of all places, the local Marine Corps Recruit Depot (MCRD).

The only men present were officers from all branches of the armed services. However, not surprisingly, local women were also encouraged to attend. It was Newport and the "Fall River Queens" all over again. Although some of the women who attended these dances were only out for "kicks," most, probably, in the back of their mind, hoped to meet someone that would result in a permanent relationship. As usual, the "horny" young men had no such altruistic motives.

The officers attending these dances were primarily interested in meeting a woman to "hook up with" the next night, Saturday. It was usually fairly easy to find a woman who was free the following evening. Having vowed not to "moon" over Randy, my long lost love, I was a regular at the MCRD on Friday night. Only once did I "strike out" and go home without a date for Saturday night, but I met no one that I wanted to see again. Late in May, that changed. I met Kathy, a woman that I thought might be "the real deal."

I have attempted not to disclose any sexual relationships that I might have had. That is partly self serving since on numerous occasions I "struck out." Eroticism is not the goal of this book. In each of my encounters with women related in this book, I will leave it to the reader's imagination the extent of my sexual involvement with each woman. There is one glaring exception. My sexual involvement with Kathy resulted in my second complete "meltdown." I will have to be graphic to describe the events that transpired.

A couple of weeks before I received orders to my permanent duty station, I met Kathy, a Navy nurse, at a Friday night dance. I was immediately attracted to her. After we danced a few dances and talked for awhile, we made a dinner date for Saturday night. The date Saturday night at first went beautifully. We had dinner at a very nice restaurant. We "hit it off" so well that I was beginning to think that this could be someone I would like to see as long as I was in the San Diego area. Who knows, it could even be possible that I might receive orders to a ship home-ported in San Diego. One never knows. After dinner, we went to a disco and danced for awhile. I took her home around midnight. I had a feeling that I was about to "get lucky."

The night progressed as I had hoped. We were soon in bed. Just as we were beginning to have sex, the headboard of her bed kept hitting the wall. Valuing her reputation with those in the adjoining apartment, she asked me to halt activities and pull the bed out from the wall. I complied. That is when everything "went south." What happened then, at one time or another, has happened to most men, but this was the first time it had happened to me. To put it bluntly, I could no longer "get it up." Nothing either of us could do could resurrect the dead. When it became evident that I was "through for the night," she acted in a way that both shocked and humiliated me. She began cursing me, demeaning my manhood, and insisted that I get dressed and leave. Shocked, I knew nothing to do but comply. I quickly dressed and sort of "slinked" out of her apartment.

I was devastated. I questioned my own manhood. As I drove back to the base, I took turns cursing her and cursing myself. When I got back to the BOQ, I went straight to bed and tried to forget what had happened. Of course, I couldn't. I had a hard time getting to sleep. I kept hoping that I would awake in the morning and find that this was all just a dream. Maybe tomorrow morning things would not seem so bleak.

When I awoke the next morning, I knew that I was in trouble. I was shell-shocked. I felt like a walking zombie. I kept staring blankly at the ceiling. At the time, I was oblivious to what was wrong, but I was, of course, in a state of deep depression. This depression was far worse than the "meltdown" in the winter of 1963. This depressive episode lasted about three months and grew more severe and debilitating as time went by. One thing that made it worse was the fact that I could not just quit and go home as I had done while in college. Somehow, I had find some way to persevere.

Each day seemed endless. I yearned for the night to come, when I could just go to my room in the BOQ and lay in bed, escaping from the world. My focus and concentration were completely shot. Each day was worse than the day before. Previously, I had anxiously awaited orders to my permanent duty station. Now I dreaded it. I just wished that I could spend my entire Navy years in the "make-work" atmosphere of my present assignment. How could I be effective anywhere? How could I survive the rigors on a Navy ship?

Soon, my orders came. I was to report for three weeks of "survival training," then a week at a "cargo handling" school in San Francisco, then off to Vietnam. In Vietnam I was to be responsible for off-loading of supplies at the deep water pier in Danang. I did not fear going to Vietnam. I feared that I was "losing my mind." I also wondered if I could "fake it" enough to carry out this assignment. I soon found out that I could not.

The next week I boarded a bus for Camp Pendleton and training in all kinds of military weapons. Even though I was not likely to face the enemy in a firefight, everyone going to Vietnam had to "be prepared" for every eventuality. While at Camp Pendleton, my mental state went from bad to worse. About the third day of the week of training I developed a severe pain in my back. Although, obviously, the pain was a by-product of my depression, the pain was real to me. I knew that if I survived this week, I could not go on any further. I had to take desperate action.

We returned to San Diego Friday afternoon. Saturday morning, I went to the Naval Hospital in San Diego and convinced the doctor on duty that I was suffering from severe pain. I became a patient of the hospital. The hospital was a sanctuary for me. I was in denial about my mental state, but at least nothing was expected of me in the hospital. Being the only officer who was a patient, I was assigned a private room. Down the hall was a group of enlisted men who bunked together in one room. I really cared about nothing or no one. I just relished the security of the hospital and not having to "fake it" anymore. Not wishing to be considered an "elitist officer snob," I spent a couple of hours each day in the enlisted men's room watching television. I had no idea what was on the television. I just stared blankly at the screen.

Most of the time, hour after hour, I was in my room playing solitaire. I could do so without really having to think. Thinking was the last thing I was capable of doing. I went to bed early. Knowing the next day would bring no challenges, I slept like a baby. Of course, during the day, the hospital ran extensive tests of all kinds to determine the source of the back pain. All proved negative. After three weeks of heaven in my sanctuary, the hospital doctors reached a conclusion. Whatever the source of my back pain, it was not serious or life threatening. Much to my dismay, I was released from the hospital.

Mercifully, the Navy waived the final two weeks of my survival training. I knew I could not have made it through that rigorous course in my present state of mind. Otherwise, the orders were the same. I was to report immediately to San Francisco for a week's training in cargo handling, then off to Vietnam. My grandfather had taught me to love my country and respond honorably when asked to answer my country's call. I would do my best to honor his memory and his admonition to "always do what's right." Somehow, I would make it.

I drove up to San Francisco and settled in the BOQ at the local Navy facility. The first day in the cargo handling class I realized it was 1963 all over again. When I had attended my college classes in the winter quarter 1963, I could recall nothing. I realized that after an intense day of schooling, I could not remember the first thing about cargo handling. I tried the second day of classes. Same result. What on earth was I to do?

That night I got a call from my mother. I knew something was wrong, for my mother often wrote but never called. She informed me that her mother, after sixteen years in a nursing home mumbling over and over again, "I can't get no better," had finally died. My mother asked me if I could attend the funeral. I did not tell her of the hell I was going through. I merely apologized that I could not attend. I also said, "Besides, my grandmother died sixteen years ago". My mother said nothing, but I knew she understood.

I knew I could not "fake it" any longer. Not only was I in a deteriorating mental state but the pain in my back was growing worse. The next day I did not report for the cargo handling class, but instead went to the Naval Hospital in Oakland. Of course, I did not mention my mental state but only reported the excruciating pain in my back. The hospital entered me as a patient. Once again, I was successful in withdrawing from a world too horrifying to face.

This was essentially same song, second verse. The hospital, just like the hospital in San Diego, began performing extensive tests to determine the source of my back pain. As in San Diego, the hospital in Oakland served as my refuge from the world. Although I hardly slept when I was in the "outside world," I again slept soundly every night. Again, I kept mainly to myself, playing endless games of solitaire. One difference between the hospital in San Diego and the hospital in Oakland was that in Oakland officers had a wing to themselves. I was the only young officer present. The others were retired officers, mostly seventy years of age or above. For the first ten days or so in the hospital, none of this made any difference. I was mainly concerned with myself.

Miraculously, one day after I had been in the hospital about two weeks, I awoke one morning with the sense that I saw a glimmer of hope. I recalled that in the winter of 1963 my mental state had spontaneously, without medical treatment, gotten better day by day. Could this be happening again? Was there a ray of hope? From that day on, each day seemed a little less frightening. My thinking, though far from normal, seemed to be less muddled each day. To a limited extent, I could begin to focus and concentrate once more on things other than myself. Maybe I could make it. I began to venture to the lounge where the older retired officers "hung out." I heard many tales of "daring do" from these "old salts."

These aging officers had served early in the century when the Navy often resembled the Navy of John Paul Jones in Revolutionary War times, when the "ships were wood and the men were iron." Many of these officers had seen service in the days of "gunboat diplomacy" when U.S. Navy ships were in constant conflict with the warlords in China. Their tales were "mind boggling" to a "young upstart" like me. I had always thought the movie *The Sand Pebbles* was all fiction. Now, I knew better.

My "recovery" was beginning to come just in the nick of time. The doctors apparently had given up on finding any medical cause for my back pain. Actually, as day by day I began to be less depressed, not surprisingly, the back pain also began to subside. By that time, I imagine the doctors had probably concluded that I was either a "slacker," hoping to avoid service in Vietnam or a "head case." Of course, the latter evaluation would have been accurate. Nevertheless I received new orders. I was to report, within days, to the USS *Frontier* (AD-25), a Destroyer Tender home-ported in Long Beach, California.

By the time I was released from the hospital, I felt that I was "halfway home" in my recovery from depression. If only I could make it for two or three weeks on the *Frontier* without "screwing up," maybe, just maybe, I could survive the challenge. Contrary to my usual pessimism, I was hopeful that everything would be alright. There was one concern that I tried to push out of my consciousness, but could not. Twice I had gone to hell and back. What assurance did I have that it would not happen again? From that time forward, in the back of my mind, I always wondered if and when "the other shoe would fall."

USS *Frontier*

The drive from Oakland to Long Beach took several hours. I had plenty of time to think. This in my case is often not good. I was still not "out of the woods" with my depression. I still had difficulty focusing or concentrating on anything for an extended period of time. Would I be able to "hack it" on the *Frontier*? Could I "fake it" sufficiently for a couple of weeks until, hopefully, I was my "normal" self?

When I got to Long Beach, it was about dusk. I could have gone straight to the ship and checked in and saved a night's lodging at a local motel. However, my orders did not require me to report until the next day, so I checked into a local motel. I am not sure whether I wanted to make a "grand entrance" the following morning or just wanted to put off the inevitable as long as possible. I got little sleep that night, contemplating the day ahead.

On the drive to the ship the next morning, all decked out in my dress uniform, I rehearsed my grand entrance. I couldn't get off to a bad start by humiliating myself. Go up the gangplank, turn and salute the ensign (the American flag), then salute the OOD (Officer of the Deck), "Ensign Hamlett reporting for duty. Request permission to come aboard sir?" "Permission granted" hopefully would be the response. Then I would request that I be taken to meet my new boss, the Supply Officer.

To my amazement, everything went without a hitch. My new boss, Commander Adair, welcomed me aboard. After a little "chit-chat," he had one of the enlisted men show me to my living quarters in the officers' section of the ship. I soon settled in and assumed the role as part of the ship's company. Maybe this would not be so bad after all.

The USS *Frontier* (AD-25) seldom went to sea. In fact, it had just returned from six months in Pearl Harbor, Hawaii. It normally would spend six months in Long Beach and six months in Pearl Harbor. Since one of my fears since joining the Navy was how I would survive on a ship at sea, being prone to sea sickness, this assignment was ideal. If I were to spend my entire naval career on the *Frontier*, I would only be at sea twice a year when going between Long Beach and Hawaii. How lucky could one be?

The mission of the *Frontier* was to repair and make seaworthy the destroyers in the Pacific fleet. Three or four destroyers would be tied up alongside the *Frontier* at one time. While these ships were being repaired, the *Frontier* took care of all the needs of the destroyers' crews. As Disbursing Officer and Food Services Officer, my job would be to pay and feed the crew of the ships alongside the *Frontier*.

A ship such as the *Frontier* required a highly skilled crew. Both the officers and enlisted men must be technologically competent. Thus, many of the officers on the *Frontier* were Warrant Officers, former enlisted men with many years of naval service, who had worked their way up through the ranks. Even most of the "regular" naval officers were much older than I. There were only four young single officers on the *Frontier*.

After reporting for duty, I managed to get along fairly well as I finished recovering from my depression of the "lost summer." Each day I felt a little better. By September 1, I was my old self. I remained depression free while stationed on the *Frontier*. As one of five Supply Corps officers on the *Frontier*, my duties were limited to Disbursing Officer, paying the crew and the ship's bills, and Food Service Officer, feeding the crew.

I had a small office, which was occupied by me, three disbursing personnel and a food service record keeper. The disbursing personnel consisted of Chief Brown, a petty officer named McCabe and a raw seaman named Hollar. My food service record keeper was named Moffett. McCabe and Hollar were topnotch but my saving grace was Chief Brown. Chief Brown was probably in his late forties, old enough to be my father. He was planning his next billet, which would be his "sunset cruise," immediately before retirement. Even though he had been exposed to all the navy had to offer and I was as "green as grass," he was always deferential to me and treated me with the utmost respect. He insisted that the others in the office do likewise. With him in charge of the disbursing function, I had nothing to worry about.

As the Disbursing Officer, I was personally liable for all the cash in my safe, which normally exceeded $20,000. This was very disconcerting. If I were to come up short in my accounts, I would have to make up the shortfall from my personal assets. For some disbursing officers on other ships, the temptation of having so much cash at their fingertips was more than they could withstand. Navy Supply Corps Officers, especially Disbursing Officers, were well represented at the naval prison at Portsmouth, New Hampshire. I am proud to say that during my tenure on the *Frontier*, I never came up even one cent short in my accounts. My own integrity and Chief Brown kept me out of trouble.

I was very careful, almost obsessive, about locking my safe anytime I left the office. Nevertheless, on more than one occasion while ashore, "living it up," I had a sinking feeling in my stomach. I could not remember locking my safe. It was impossible for me to enjoy the festivities. I just had to go back and check the safe. On each such occasion, I found the safe locked. I had interrupted an enjoyable evening for nothing.

Once, I did leave my safe unlocked as I attended to other duties on the ship. When I returned to my office, the safe was locked. A few minutes later, when I had occasion to open the safe, a piece of pie was sitting on top of the cash. Chief Brown, McCabe, Hollar and Moffett could hardly contain themselves. Finally, they all let out "belly laughs." The joke was on me. I tried to be a good sport and laughed along with them. However, always playing it close to the vest and almost paranoid, when everyone had left for the day, I counted every cent and balanced the cash on hand with my records. One cannot be too careful.

I am not going to dwell on the problems I encountered as food service officer other than to say "it was a challenge." There was no strong chief, such as Chief Brown, in charge of food service. Also, I had to deal with the "messcooks." To help with the "grunt work" regarding feeding the men, such as cleaning the pots and pans, keeping the food service area clean, etc., each division on ship had to send at least one person to serve as "messcook." Each division always sent the troublemakers or the least desirable person in their division. Many times I wished I was only responsible for the disbursing function.

Captain Howell, the captain of the *Frontier*, was a four striper, the equivalent of a full bird Colonel in the other armed services. He was captain of the *Frontier* almost the entire time that I served onboard. I could not have asked for a finer leader under which to serve. Like all captains of navy ships, his wish was taken as a command. He was a stern taskmaster. Yet, he was understanding and compassionate with the crew.

Traditionally, on payday on navy ships, the Disbursing Officer goes to the Captain's cabin and pays him before paying the rest of the crew. One payday, when I went to pay Captain Howell, he was nowhere to be found. Thereafter, I got wrapped up in paying the remainder of the crew and problems in the Food Services area. It was about 3:00 o'clock in the afternoon, when I realized with horror that I had forgotten to pay the Captain. I raced to his cabin fearing retribution for such a stupid mistake. The Captain opened the door to his cabin. I apologized profusely, explaining the problems I had faced that day. The Captain just smiled and said, "That's alright, son, I understand." To my great relief, I had dodged yet another bullet.

During my time on the *Frontier*, I went to Las Vegas with friends from another ship about monthly. There was one humorous moment with regard to my first trip to Las Vegas. My boss, Commander Adair, was a nice man, but a career officer. He was responsible for everything that occurred on the *Frontier* with regard to Supply, including my assignment as Disbursing Officer. His career was in jeopardy if any of the other officers under his command got in serious trouble. When I left for Las Vegas, I left directly from the ship. The first time that I set off for Las Vegas, I met Commander Adair on the Quarterdeck as I was leaving the ship. When I told him that I was leaving for Vegas, he looked down at the overnight bag I was carrying. He said nothing but turned white as a sheet. I knew he could just see the cash in my safe and his career both going down the drain. As I left the ship, it was hard for me to suppress a smile.

Unfortunately, while our ship was in Long Beach, for two or three months the *Frontier* was the Admiral's Flagship. Spit and polish was the order of the day. I hated it when I was forced to serve as Officer of the Deck (OOD) during that period. Particularly frustrating was the obsessive-compulsive nature of the Admiral's aide, a young lieutenant with visions of one day becoming an Admiral himself. He became "stressed out" over every minor infraction, most of which the Admiral would not have noticed, or if he did, would probably have not given a damn. All the *Frontier* officers walked on egg shells, fearing committing some infraction. Fortunately, all bad things eventually come to an end. In early January we set sail for Pearl Harbor. Everyone looked forward to serving six months in Hawaii.

Once we reached Pearl Harbor in early January, everything changed for the better. The *Frontier* was moored at Ford Island across the bay from Honolulu. A ferry connecting Ford Island to Honolulu ran from 6:00 AM until 11:00 PM. Since the *Frontier* was a very large ship, the officers had been allowed to have their cars brought along on the large open deck. This was a blessing for the young single officers who wanted to often frequent Honolulu and Waikiki. The whole atmosphere on the ship changed. The entire crew, both the officers and the sailors were more "laid back." Leaving the ship in casual clothes, rather than in uniform, was permitted. Everyone gave a collective sigh of relief.

I had very little social interaction with the other junior officers while in Long Beach. However, in Hawaii, Lew Goodman, a Jewish officer from New York City, and I often "hit the beach" together. With Lew and his New York accent, and me sounding like an illiterate "redneck," we made quite the odd couple. We left the ship so often together that Commander Adair referred to us as "running mates."

As might be expected of single men in their early twenties, Lew and I were primarily interested in meeting women. Hawaii was the perfect place. Many young women from Canada and the U.S. vacationed in Hawaii, many of them seeking romance. Hawaii was the perfect place for such an endeavor. Lew and I aimed to please. Unfortunately for me, Lew was a handsome man, far better looking than I. In addition, my redneck accent sometimes worked against me. Lew often had the "pick of the litter," but there were more than enough young vacationing women to go around.

Sometimes, not wishing to compete with Lew for a young lady's affections, I set out on my own. Early on, I wandered upon a lounge that was more than any single man could hope for. The name was "Chuck's Cellar." It was located in the basement of one of the numerous hotels on Waikiki. It was small and out of the way. What made "Chuck's Cellar" such an attraction was that flight crews, with of course stewardesses, from a large international airline stayed at the hotel and frequented the lounge. Not wishing competition, I selfishly kept "Chuck's Cellar" a secret from Lew and the other officers.

Being depression free and being in paradise seemed like "heaven on earth" to me. I assumed that I would spend the rest of my commitment to the military on the *Frontier*, until I once again became a civilian in August 1969. However, things seldom go as planned. After we had been in Pearl Harbor approximately three months, we got orders to set sail for San Diego. The *Frontier* was first commissioned in World War II and had seen its best days. It was to be "decommissioned" and put into mothballs. The news knocked the wind out of the sails of the entire crew, including me. I was faced with the reality of soon being assigned to a new duty station.

I will not dwell on the almost two months I spent in San Diego while the ship was in the process of being decommissioned. My experience with Kathy even soured me on the Friday night dances at the Marine Corps Recruiting Depot. I did not do anything very exciting those two months. I was, more or less, treading water, waiting for my next assignment.

Finally, I received my orders. No later than June 4, 1968, I was to report to the U.S. Naval Support Activity, Danang, Vietnam. It was very ironic. Having once escaped service in Vietnam, I could now seek atonement. With no sign of depression, I knew this time it would be different. I had no fear of dying in Vietnam. My previous experiences with depression had turned me into a fatalist. I had stared insanity in the face and had somehow survived. Could death be worse than the fear of "losing your mind"?

I had only a brief stay home before having to report to an Air Force base near Los Angeles and the subsequent flight to Danang. My birthday was June 13. Although my family tried to be upbeat about my impending assignment, I knew they were much more fearful than was I. At any rate, three days before I was to leave, my entire extended family showed up at my parents' home for a combination birthday party and "going away party." They went all out with tons of food, fireworks, the works. I could tell from the way they looked at me that they wondered if they would ever see me again. On the surface, there were smiles all round, but I could sense an undercurrent of fear.

The next day, two days before my departure, I received a wedding announcement in the mail. I suddenly felt like someone had ripped my heart out. Randy had married someone else. I was surprised at my reaction to the news; however, I should not have been surprised at the news. Our letters to each other had been increasingly infrequent. Nevertheless, she had been my first love and I still thought of her as the "love of my life." I had been with several women since last seeing Randy, but none of them meant anything to me. However, that day I vowed to get on with my life and try to forget her for yet a second time. It was probably good that I would have a year in Vietnam to "get her out of my system."

It was around the first of June that my family took me to the airport to see me off. My sister, Sandra, then fifteen, and my mother wept as they said good-bye. My two brothers were too young to understand exactly what was happening. My father, who usually showed no emotion, seemed to stifle a tear as he said good-bye and offered his advice: "Don't be no hero."

Vietnam

I had expected to have a fairly boring four-hour flight from Nashville to Los Angeles. Was I in for a surprise! I had decided to fly first class rather than coach. Why not? It was possible that there might never be a return trip home. I also wore my dress khaki uniform. I wanted to leave in style.

I set down in a window seat in first class. As usual, the flight crew was scurrying about the plane, when a stunning stewardess suddenly sat down in the aisle seat beside me. I was confused but grateful. It seems she was "deadheading" on the flight to Los Angeles. She was a mere passenger. The next morning she was to catch an international flight to Tokyo.

The trip to Los Angeles seemed like twenty minutes, not four hours. We talked, laughed and had a bit too much wine during the trip. We also agreed to "hook up" in Los Angeles after the plane landed. What a night to remember. I later realized she probably just felt sorry for me going off to war and was just doing her patriotic duty. I could not have cared less about her motive. At any rate, I almost missed my flight to Vietnam the next morning. What a way to go off to war!

I do not remember much of the flight to Danang. I slept much of the way. After the plane landed in Danang, for some reason of which I am not quite sure, I was to spend my first night "in country" at a military hotel in downtown Danang. My first reaction to being in Vietnam was shock. Most of the local Vietnamese were decked out in black. I had previously had the impression that black was the color of the Viet Cong. It took a while for me to get used to the fact that black was the universal dress of the Vietnamese people.

The next morning, an officer from the Naval Supply Depot picked me up and took me to the compound where I would live for the next year. On the way, we crossed over the bridge separating "our part" of Danang from the city of Danang itself. Marines were stationed every few yards on the bridge, firing at just about anything that moved in the river below. The reason for this precaution was that in the past the bridge had once been blown up. After crossing the bridge, we drove four or five miles before reaching the compound I would call home. After I got settled into my sleeping quarters, I was issued "Marine Green" uniforms, steel plated boots and a .45 caliber handgun, which I would be required to carry anytime I left the compound.

The next day I went to the Supply Depot and reported for duty. I was to be one of several inventory control officers at the depot. My specific responsibility was to oversee several highly educated enlisted men, as well as some young Vietnamese girls, in keeping up with the supplies on hand at the depot. This was a very important responsibility. Heaven forbid we should run out of some essential war materials. It is hard to imagine the immense size of the Supply Depot. When I reported in the summer of 1968, there were approximately 650,000 American troops in all of Vietnam. About 200,000 of them were stationed in the northern part of Vietnam. Our depot was responsible for providing the 200,000 military personnel in the north with needed supplies. At that time, the U.S. Naval Support Activity in Danang was the largest such facility in the world.

There is a recurring theme in my life. Sooner or later I will endure yet another depressive episode. Shortly after arriving in Vietnam, I realized such an episode was "coming on." This episode did not seem to me to be the forerunner of another "meltdown." Perhaps I could "gut it out" for a short period and live through this episode without anyone becoming aware.

Overall Danang was safe: however, not everything was "rosy." During daylight hours, the enemy disappeared into the "woodwork." At night, they resurfaced, often with a vengeance. At night, the enemy "crept up" close enough to Danang to "toss in" a few mortars or fire a few Russian-made missiles. This did not happen but about once every week or ten days; however, it happened often enough to be perplexing.

The most disturbing incident that happened that year came one night, in the middle of the night, when I was abruptly awakened by a large "boom." Several miles away at an off-loading point for Navy ships, some form of enemy ordnance had a "direct hit" on a fully loaded ammunition ship. The remains of the sailors onboard were never found. A large chunk of the bow of the ship was found a few hundred yards on the surrounding land mass.

It was not unusual for the alert to sound that there was "incoming," usually the Russian-made missiles. Everyone would take to their respective bunkers. Usually the missiles landed harmlessly, but occasionally they would hit an important target. A couple of times, missiles landed in the Supply Depot compound.

While I was in Vietnam, the one big "hit" the enemy was successful in making near the Supply Depot involved the South Vietnamese Army, the people we were, supposedly, in Vietnam to help. The South Vietnamese had an ammunition dump adjacent to the Supply Depot. Unfortunately, they sometimes played "fast and loose" with both safety concerns and common sense, sometimes leaving live ammunition on top of the ground instead of safely underground. One night, an enemy ordnance of some sort hit its mark. The result was continuous explosions for two or three days. I was not on duty at the Supply Depot that night but those who were remained stranded there a couple of days, confined to their bunkers, until the "fireworks display" was over. No one could enter or leave the depot. The bombardment not only destroyed the South Vietnamese ammunition facility but "wrecked havoc" on the Supply Depot. Fortunately, to my knowledge, there were no injuries to American personnel.

There was one incident involving incoming missiles that had its humorous aspects. One day federal auditors arrived to audit the books of the Supply Depot. Being an auditor myself and knowing the enormous material transactions at the depot, I anticipated a lengthy audit. As luck would have it, on their first night in Danang as the auditors were snug in their beds, a missile landed squarely on one of our enlisted men's barracks, not far from where the auditors slept. Fortunately, all the enlisted men were safely in their bunker when the missile hit. No one was injured. In my year in Danang, that was the first and only time that a missile had a direct hit on a barracks in our compound. The next day the auditors informed us that they had completed their audit and were catching the first plane out. Some audit!

I had accurately diagnosed the depressive episode I was undergoing immediately after arriving in Vietnam. It was not a complete "meltdown" like 1963 and 1967. Unfortunately, this depressive episode did not only last a couple of weeks but for the better part of two months. As usual, I had difficulty "focusing" or "concentrating." My ability to "think" was compromised. I was just trying to "muddle through" until the depression passed. I realized that even though I was doing my best, I was in, in fact, an ineffectual officer. I was sure that all this was not lost on my superiors.

As had happened in the past, eventually I could feel the depression "letting up." Each day was better than the day before. I was becoming myself once more. Unfortunately, the damage had been done. After about two months, I was transferred to a new job, to be in charge of the food storage facilities on the depot. No one gave any reason for the transfer. No one complained to me that my performance had been substandard. I surmise "the Brass" just decided that I was just in over my head. Given my mental state, they were right.

My new responsibility was "Storage Officer," in charge of six large warehouses of food stuffs and a large "hardstand" where row upon row of "C Rations" were stored. Also, I had to oversee the offloading of food items transported from the "deep water pier" and the withdrawals of food items by military units from the warehouse. Even though a "downgrade" from the inventory control job, it was still a position of considerable responsibility.

The "kicker" in this new job was that I also was to oversee the shipment of milk and ice cream products from the milk plant on the compound to the troops out in the "boonies." Sound easy? Think again. If for any reason, a shipment of ice cream or milk did not go out on time, all hell broke loose. Sometimes the "brass" got involved. No excuse was acceptable.

Even though I assigned two of my best men to give twenty-four-hour "coverage" at the milk plant, much of my time was spent ensuring that there were no "foul-ups."

I was not immune from heartrending experiences. Our Supply Depot donated anything we could spare to a Catholic-run orphanage on the outskirts of Danang. I was responsible for coordinating the efforts to assist the sisters who ran the orphanage. I visited it quite often. I became friends with the sister who was in charge of the orphanage. One would have to be callous beyond belief not to be depressed by the conditions at the orphanage. Most of the children were very young, many of them babies, lying in individual beds in the open air, covered only by an awning in case of rain. The sisters did their best to "shew away" the abundance of flies present in the orphanage compound.

It was immediately obvious that almost all of the babies and older children were of mixed racial parentage. Obviously, the mothers were Vietnamese and the fathers American. It was also obvious that about half had white fathers and the other half black fathers. As biracial children, fathered by the hated Americans, these children would never have a place in Vietnamese society. *What would be their fate?* I pondered. Every time I visited the orphanage, I tried to keep my emotions in check. I did not want the sisters to know the heartache I felt.

We had nightly movies on the compound where food and drink were served by young Vietnamese girls. As we watched the movies, I could not help but observe the look on the faces of the young Vietnamese girls. When an American home was shown on the screen, the young girls stared in awe. Living their lives of poverty across the river, they could not relate to what they saw. Since the Communists took over all of Vietnam in the mid-seventies, I have not helped but ponder the fate of these young girls and all other Vietnamese who had "fraternized" with the Americans. I am sure there was a heavy price to pay. I have tried, to no avail, to push such thoughts from my mind.

Something happened to me one day on a trip to China Beach that was not all that unusual. I was stopped in a congested area, waiting for the traffic to clear. My truck having no air conditioning, my driver's side window was rolled down. Negligently, I placed my arm upon the open window. Out of nowhere, came a young Vietnamese boy, no older than twelve or thirteen, who grabbed the watch on my left arm and yanked. The chain link band broke and off he ran through the village with my watch. Startled, instinctively, I reached for the .45 on my hip, but almost immediately came to my senses and reholstered my weapon. It was, after all, only a watch. It meant much more to the young boy than it did to me.

As I took one day at a time, the days turned into weeks, the weeks into months. Soon, I was a "short-timer." As May 1969 arrived, I could almost "feel the civilian life." Even though my three-year commitment did not officially end until August 19, 1969, the Navy was "cutting me some slack." My orders said that as soon as I left Vietnam and arrived back in the "world," I was to report to Long Beach, my old stomping ground, for "out-processing." I had requested permission to delay reporting to Long Beach for thirty days. Permission granted. My reporting date in Long Beach was changed to late June. Soon I would be leaving the Navy, but first I wanted a chance to see an Asia at peace. I could hardly wait until the end of May when I would once and for all leave the war behind me. Surely nothing could happen now to sabotage my soaring spirits.

But I could not leave well enough alone. I was my own worst enemy. Each officer completing his active duty commitment was sent a form on which to evaluate his experience in the Navy. Most officers were so happy to be leaving the military that they just "blew it off" and said little or nothing on the form.

Foolishly, I diligently tried to be honest in my evaluation of my military service. Unfortunately, some of my comments were uncomplimentary to the Navy. One theme in my evaluation was that the Navy treated enlisted men like children, from the demeaning enlisted "sailor suit" to the condescending manner in which enlisted men were addressed by their superiors. I included a laundry list of improvements that I thought should be made. I should have known better.

A few days later, I received word that the Captain in charge of the entire Supply operation in Danang wished to see me at an appointed time. Why had I been so stupid? Why had I not just kept my opinions to myself? What possible good could come from being honest? But, alas, I had to face the music. The boat trip across the river to the Captain's office went much too quickly. As I sat in the Captain's outer office waiting to be summoned, I was sick at heart. As usual, anticipation was much worse than realization. The Captain greeted me cordially with a few offhand remarks to break the ice. He then asked me to explain my comments on the evaluation form. I was trapped. If I "back-peddled," I would appear to be a wimp. Yet, I had to choose my words carefully. After I had explained my comments, I awaited the wrath of "God." To the contrary, the Captain just smiled and said, "Son, when I was a junior officer, I probably had some of those same thoughts." He dismissed me with no further comment. Miraculously, I had dodged yet another bullet.

On my last day in Danang, my boss, LTCDR Bowne drove me to the airport. My plan was to spend about a week each in Thailand, Hong Kong, Taiwan and Japan, then off to Long Beach to become a civilian once more. As I have stated before, it is good that God does not allow one to see the future. Within six weeks, I would begin a slow descent to hell in yet another "meltdown." This complete "meltdown" would last almost nine months and make the meltdowns in 1963 and 1967 seem like a walk in the park. This time, it would almost cost me my life. But that was several weeks in the future. For now, I was off to explore Asia. I could not have been happier.

6

Transition to Civilian Life

Exploring Asia

I did not leave Vietnam directly from Danang. I first had to fly to Saigon and spend the night. From Saigon, I chose to fly on commercial airlines at my own expense during the entire trip rather than fly standby on military aircraft. I left Saigon early one morning via Thai International. Upon arriving in Bangkok, I chose to stay at an upscale hotel. Having spent little in my year in Vietnam, money was no object. I had saved almost my entire paycheck, including hostile fire pay. Also, unlike today, travel in Asia in the '60s, for Americans, was relatively inexpensive.

Most of my time in Thailand was spent in the Bangkok area. Although I did take two or three tours to outlying areas, most of my time was spent "vegging out" at the hotel pool. At the pool, I met many interesting people from throughout the world. A couple of times I had dinner with people I met at the pool but usually I dined alone.

After a week or more in Bangkok, I decided it was time to move on. I boarded the plane for Hong Kong, not knowing that in Hong Kong I would have an experience which I would wistfully recall the rest of my life. Upon arriving in Hong Kong, I abandoned my extravagant manner and rented a "cubby hole" in a low-rent but safe hotel. The room contained only a bed, a lamp and a chest of drawers. It did not matter. Considering Hong Kong's reputation for excitement, I had planned to spend very little time in my room. As it turned out, I spent even less time than I had expected.

My first full day in Hong Kong, I spent the entire day exploring the city. I was overwhelmed with the activity. In 1969, Hong Kong remained a British Crown Colony. Later, in the '90s, the lease of Hong Kong from China would expire and Hong Kong would revert to China. But in 1969, it was an interesting combination of the Chinese culture and British aristocracy, although populated primarily by the Chinese.

The hotel in which I was staying was in Kowloon, across the bay from Hong Kong itself. That first day, after exploring both Kowloon and Hong Kong, I found myself on the ferry from Hong Kong to Kowloon. I sat on the first row of a bench on the ferry. I noticed sitting on the other end of the bench one of the most beautiful women that I had ever seen. I was enthralled. I tried to look straight ahead but found myself averting my eyes in her direction. There was no way that I would have thought of approaching her. She was clearly "out of my league." When the ferry trip ended, I watched her disappear into the crowd, never expecting to see her again.

On my second day in Hong Kong, I signed up for a tour of the "new territories." The new territories were part of the British possession, but were far outside the bustling city. The area was largely unpopulated. The appeal of this tour was the opportunity to "peer" into Communist China, at that time both a threat and an enigma to the western world. I had expected a quiet day before exploring the "bar district" of Hong Kong that night. I took my seat, the fourth seat back on the left side of the tour bus. The bus was almost empty because few people had chosen to take this tour.

A couple of minutes later, I glanced up and entering the bus was my "fantasy woman" from the ferry the previous day.

My heart palpitated, hoping against hope that she would choose to sit beside me. Of course, as I had expected, she did not. However, she did choose to sit immediately behind me. After a few minutes of silence, I took out my "state of the art" camera that I had purchased in Hong Kong the previous day for a ridiculously low price. As I fumbled with the camera, which was much too sophisticated for me, I heard a voice from behind me say: "What a nice camera, do you mind if I see it?" Startled, I started to hand the camera over the back of my seat to her when she said: "That's alright. I will just move up there." I thought I would faint.

During the tour, I noticed little of the "sights," even "Red China." Her name was Gaye. My mind raced ahead at the possibilities. I asked her to have dinner with me that night. Surprisingly, she accepted. At one point she asked me if I had visited the "bar district" since I had arrived in Hong Kong. Thankfully, I could honestly say that I had not, although, in truth, that had been my original intention that very night.

The next four days were one of the highlights of my life. We were almost constant companions until she left for Tokyo on June 14th. We explored the city by day, had fantastic dinners, and just enjoyed each other's company. It being obvious that she was wealthier than me, she insisted that we share the costs of our endeavors. My original plan had been to fly to Taiwan on June 16. After I met Gaye, I decided to leave for Taiwan on the fourteenth, the same day she was to leave for Tokyo. I knew anything that happened to me in Hong Kong after she left would be anti-climatic.

Gaye was an enigma. She would not even tell me her last name. About the only thing she revealed was that Hong Kong was the third leg on a "round the world" trip that would last six months. Although she was obviously wealthy, I did not pry into the source of her wealth. I asked no questions about her personal life. She volunteered little information. I decided just to enjoy her company and let "sleeping dogs lie." This was no time to "rock the boat." I did not want to spoil a good thing by being inquisitive.

In contrast to my "cubby hole," Gaye had a nice suite in an upscale hotel, where we spent most of our time when not exploring the city. Although careful not to pry into Gaye's personal life, I maintained an inquisitive mindset. The second day after we met, while in Gaye's suite, I had noticed a portfolio lying on the back of a table in an obscure part of her suite. Instinctively, I sensed that this portfolio could answer some of the unanswered questions that I had about Gaye. I said nothing about my inquisitive nature to Gaye. I just waited for the opportunity to see what secrets lay inside that portfolio.

On the third day of our time together, I got the opportunity for which I had waited. Gaye said that she needed to run a couple of errands and would be back in a few minutes. Here was my chance. As soon as she had had time to leave the building, I went over and examined the portfolio. As I turned the pages, I was astounded. Page after page was Gaye's photo on the cover of major magazines. In the back were copies of full page advertisements featuring Gaye advertising an assortment of products. At last, I knew the secret of her prosperity.

Soon my shock turned to panic. What if Gaye returned unexpectedly and caught me uncovering her secret? I knew it would be curtains for our adventure. I immediately replaced the portfolio exactly where it had been and returned to the couch where I had been sitting when she had left. Fortunately for me, when Gaye returned she did not suspect a thing. Of course, for the rest of our time together I remained mum.

There was one aspect of our four days together that, upon reflection, should have given me pause. Even though we took numerous photos on our excursions throughout Hong Kong, many including pictures of me, Gaye always refused to let me take a picture of her. At first, I had assumed that she was just camera shy. After examining the portfolio, I realized the reason for her reticence at having her picture taken. On our last day in Hong Kong, she finally consented to letting me take one snapshot of her. I have kept that snapshot throughout the years to remind me of one of the most exciting times in my life. Without that photo, I would probably question whether or not the entire episode was a figment of my imagination.

After celebrating my twenty-sixth birthday on June 13, the next day Gaye and I left for the airport together. Our farewell was somewhat strange for two people who had shared so much in our short stay in Hong Kong. At the airport, there was no exchanging of phone numbers or addresses or promises of future contact. We both realized that we had just been "two ships passing in the night" and that we would never have any contact or see each other again. A simple kiss and she was off to Tokyo. A few minutes later, I boarded the plane for Taiwan. Knowing Gaye did wonders for my self-esteem that had always been suspect. I suspected that Taiwan and, later, Japan, would just be afterthoughts. I was right about Taiwan but definitely wrong about Japan.

The week I spent in Tiawan was very relaxing but not noteworthy. I was off to Tokyo. When I arrived in Tokyo, I checked into a nice but moderately priced hotel. Although Tokyo in the '60s was inexpensive by today's standards, it was more expensive than the other countries that I had visited. In contrast to my very boring visit to Taiwan, Tokyo was an exciting place to visit. I spent many exciting days and nights exploring the city.

Before I left Vietnam, I had made a pact with Chris, a fellow naval officer in Danang, to meet him in Tokyo in late June while he was there on a week's R & R. Unfortunately, our timing was a bit flawed. By the time Chris arrived in Tokyo, I had but three days left before I had to return stateside for out processing from the Navy. There was method in Chris's desire to meet me in Tokyo. Chris's fiancée, Sue and her roommate, Gloria were to meet him in Tokyo while the two women were vacationing in Asia. My purpose in meeting the three of them in Tokyo was to "take care" of Gloria while Chris romanced his fiancée, Sue. To do Chris a favor, I agreed to this plan. What did I have to lose? He would have done the same for me.

On the pre-arranged night, I met Chris, Sue and Gloria for dinner. Gloria and I immediately "hit it off." "Taking care" of Gloria was certainly going to be a pleasure, not a chore. Gloria and I had a wonderful time for the rest of my time in Tokyo. The four of us explored the city by day. At night, the two couples went their separate ways, just as Chris had hoped. Everybody was happy. I was only sorry that my time with Gloria was to be so short.

After our brief time together, I said good-bye to the three of them and headed for the Air Force base and my trip home. I never expected to see any of them again. Once again, I had met a woman that I really liked but separation came much too soon. But in one's life, fate often takes strange twists and turns. Since that day in late June 1969, I have never seen Chris again. However, little did I know that within six weeks I would see Sue and Gloria again, although the circumstances would not be filled with joy and happiness as in Tokyo but, for me, with a sense of bewilderment.

When I arrived back in "the World," I first landed in San Francisco. I then took a flight to Los Angeles. Late that night, I checked into the Naval Station at Long Beach, from where I was to be discharged a few days later. I lived in the BOQ for several days during out processing. During my trip through Asia, I had been in denial. I thought the trip would last forever. Now, I was faced with the stark reality that a new phase of my life was about to begin. It scared the hell out of me. What would my future be? During those few days, I watched television a lot but my mind was a million miles away. I guess the uncertainty of my future and the magnitude of the decisions that must be made was more than my fragile psyche could handle. Reluctantly, I came to realize that I was encountering a "depressive episode." I tried to tell myself that this episode would be short-lived like so many in the past. But that was not to be. It was the beginning of a complete "meltdown," far worse than those in 1963 and 1967.

Facing the Future

It was around the first of July 1969 when I arrived home in Nashville. Of course, there was a happy homecoming celebration with all of my family. Everyone was ecstatic that I had survived a year in Vietnam unscathed. The first week that I was home I did very little. Two or three times that week I did "hang out" with my family at the pool at the poor man's country club to which my family belonged. Life should have been grand for me.

I was in denial that my current depressive state was anything but the "two week" variety which I had suffered several times before. Surely, soon my mind would once again function properly and I would be able to escape the "muddled thinking" I was enduring. Surely, my ability to focus and concentrate would return. Surely, I was not headed for another "meltdown." But once more, the simplest tasks seemed like major hurdles. However, I was good, as always, at "faking it" and making everyone think that I was "normal."

I thought that, perhaps, if I could land a job, everything would be fine. Wishfully thinking that I would soon be myself again, I arranged for two job interviews during my third week home. Both interviews were a disaster. I knew that my resume looked better than most and that I was well qualified for the positions sought. However, during the interviews, my demeanor was such that it must have been obvious that "something was just not right." I did not hear back from either company. I did not blame them. In my heart of hearts, I realized that even if I had been hired by either company, I could not possibly have performed the job requirements in my current state of mind. At last, I admitted to myself that I was in trouble.

Yet, even though I am a pessimist by nature, hope sprang eternal when faced with desperation. Irrationally, I finally decided that returning to Charlotte would cure all my ills. After all, the summer of 1965 and the winter of 1966 had been among the most pleasant in my life. I knew that Randy was now married, but what did that matter? In the summer of '65, I had really enjoyed Charlotte even before I had had my relationship with Randy. Also, the CPA firm with which I worked in the winter of 1966 had really been impressed with my work and hated that I had to leave to fulfill my obligation to the Navy. I knew that they would welcome me back.

In the latter part of July, I called my former employer in Charlotte and informed them that I wished to return to work. I was a bit embarrassed because I had had no contact with anyone in the firm since I left in April 1966, over three years before. Nevertheless, they seemed thrilled that I wished to return. They asked if I would be able to report by August 1. I eagerly agreed. My family was not exactly thrilled by my decision to return to Charlotte. They had assumed that I would stay in Nashville. I could not tell them that nobody in Nashville would probably hire me and that returning to Charlotte was a last desperate chance to save my future. I knew that I had no other options. I could only pray that the curse of depression would disappear before I had to prove myself in Charlotte.

Even before I left Nashville for Charlotte, the euphoria of "solving my problem" soon wore off. Reality reared its ugly head. I had been depressed for about a month. This was no "two week episode." I feared that this was the "real thing."

Rather than beginning to come out of my depression, if anything, I was getting worse. Was this another complete "meltdown?" These thoughts only intensified the depression. But the "die was cast." Off to Charlotte I would go, come hell or high water. I had sold my '56 Chevy before I had gone to Vietnam. Anyway, an ordinary car would not carry all of my possessions. I had loaded up on bargains while in Hong Kong and had shipped them all home. In late July, I rented a van, packed all my belongings and was ready to "set sail" for Charlotte. As I said good-bye to my family, I had difficulty holding back the tears. I tried my best to put on my "happy face" and appear optimistic about my future. But inside, I was dying. What would be my fate? Would I ever see my family again? I got into the van and drove off. By the time I reached the end of the driveway, I burst into tears. Only God could save me now.

Falling Apart

My trip to Charlotte consisted of one part crying and one part planning my next move once I arrived in Charlotte. I had always been an organizer, with obsessive compulsive tendencies, never leaving anything to chance. By the time I reached Charlotte, it was almost dark. I checked into a motel and made a list of things to accomplish the next day. I could not waste any time if I was to be settled in by the time I reported for work. Late that night, I watched *The Tonight Show* with Johnny Carson. I stared at the screen blankly. Nothing seemed funny those days.

Early the next morning, I started my search for an apartment. When I had been in Charlotte in 1966, I had known of a "swinging" apartment complex with mostly young single people. Even though I was not exactly in a swinging mood, I went to the complex to see if they had any vacancies. Fortunately they did. I rented an apartment, unloaded all my belongings from the van, and then turned in the van at the local rental agency. I then took a taxi to a local Mercury dealer. In no time at all, I had purchased a bright red 1969 Mercury Cougar. I paid cash. I still had quite a stash left over from Vietnam. I had not been in a bartering mood. I made little effort to get the salesman to lower the price. I am sure that I got "taken to the cleaners." But what did it really matter? Money was the least of my worries.

Having accomplished my primary goals, I settled in at my apartment for the weekend, waiting to report to my employer on Monday. I met several residents at the pool that weekend. They gave me a warm greeting. However, I had trouble getting my mind off what to expect when I reported for work on Monday. During both Saturday and Sunday, the residents of the apartment had a combination "beer fest" and volleyball game in the pool. In the frivolities of those afternoons, I almost, but not quite, forgot my troubles. You don't have to do much thinking to play volleyball. Temporarily, I thought that maybe I was getting better. But then night came. In the loneliness of the apartment, my depression came flooding back. As usual those days, I slept little Sunday night. I prayed that somehow I would get so involved in work that the depression would go away. If not, what would happen to me?

I reported for work Monday morning. Even though I had been gone for over three years, there were many familiar faces. Everyone seemed happy to have me back. They welcomed me almost as a hero for having served in Vietnam. I was very surprised, for my previous contact with civilians since I had returned from Vietnam had been far less welcoming. Like others who served in Vietnam, I had often been treated as though I had betrayed my country by serving in Vietnam.

I found that many of the young auditors I knew in 1966 had moved up the ladder and now held more responsible positions. When I was later assigned to audits, many of my contemporaries in 1966 were now auditors in charge, my bosses. Had

I not been preoccupied with my own mental problems, I might have wondered whether or not, by serving my country, I had somehow fallen behind in my professional development. But I gave little thought to that. I had graver concerns. I wondered whether in my present mental state I could actually do an adequate job. I knew, deep inside, that I couldn't.

Fortunately, I found that the first week required little thought. I just "hung out" in the office and got familiar with present practices and procedures of the firm. It was just, basically, a "settling in" period. I also learned that the following three weeks I would be in training at the firm training facility in Chicago. I hoped against hope that I could somehow make it through those three weeks of training satisfactorily and, that when I reported to my first assignment thereafter, I would be "my old self." I had to hope that somehow everything would work out. If I failed at this job, what would happen to me?

The following Sunday I flew to Chicago and settled into a dorm room on the Chicago campus of Northwestern University. The university's students were away for the summer and my firm, which had offices throughout the country, annually used the facilities to hold its training sessions. When I left Chris, Sue and Gloria in Tokyo in June, I had never expected to see any of them again. Yet, here I was in Chicago, where Sue and Gloria lived. Chris, of course, had returned to Vietnam to finish out his tour. As soon as I arrived, I called Gloria. She seemed excited to hear my voice. She invited me over Monday night after my first day of classes. Of course, I accepted.

The three weeks of classes would have been grueling for anyone. In my case, it was torture. There was non-stop instruction in auditing practices and procedures from early in the morning until late afternoon. At night, there were study sessions in the early evening. I found the classes next to impossible to navigate. With my problems with focusing and concentration,

I felt I was hopelessly in over my head. I was doing my best, but I knew my work was inadequate.

At the beginning of the third week, an instructor from the Charlotte office who was supposed to monitor the work of the new auditors from the Charlotte office, "called me out." In a nice way, he informed me that my work was sub-par. What could I do but promise to put in more time on my work and strive to do better. The third week, I did work later at night but it was hopeless. I am not sure whether or not the instructor ever reported my inadequate performance during those three weeks to the "big bosses" in Charlotte. If he did, no one in the Charlotte office chastised me or even mentioned the training session when I returned.

I could not have made it through the three weeks were it not for the sanctuary I found at Sue's and Gloria's almost every night I was in Chicago. Sometimes it was late when I arrived at their apartment because of the night study sessions; however, I was always welcomed, especially by Gloria. Even when I arrived early in the evening, Sue soon "made herself scarce," retreating to her bedroom, ostensibly to read. Gloria and I snuggled on the couch and watched television until about midnight when I would return to my dorm room. Temporarily, I retreated from the real world and put my troubles in the back of my mind.

I am sure to Gloria's surprise, I made no sexual overtures. Even in this safe haven, the depression was always there. I almost never had any interest in sex when in a depressed state. Around midnight, when I returned to my dorm room, the real world once again descended upon me. For me, it was another sleepless night, wondering how I could possibly make it through the next day. Somehow, I always did. Somehow, I made it through all three weeks.

After I finished the three weeks of training in Chicago, I was assigned to a series of small audits in the months of September and October. Each audit lasted only two or three weeks. I was, of course, the junior auditor on the job and was not involved with major audit issues. Thank God for that. My work was essentially "grunt work" which most junior auditors could do standing on their head. Not so for me. Try as I might, I could not adequately do the simplest of tasks. My "fuzzy thinking" and inability to focus or concentrate doomed me to failure at even the most rudimentary tasks.

More than once, an auditor in charge corrected me or made reference to mistakes that I was making. I believe that these auditors in charge failed to communicate to the "higher ups" the futility of dealing with me and my inadequate performance. Knowing how the "system" works, this is probably not surprising. Each auditor in charge, himself, was on the spot. Any failure of a subordinate to perform adequately might reflect not only on the subordinate himself but on the in-charge auditor's leadership ability. Each in-charge auditor for which I worked probably was just glad to get rid of me after a couple of weeks and hoped that I would never be assigned to him again.

Even though I was never "taken to task" or reprimanded by one of the "big bosses," I was completely aware of my failures. I knew the day of reckoning would eventually come. Where was this all going to end? What was to become of me? While lying in bed late one Sunday night around the first of November, I knew what I had to do. The world was too much for me to bare. I had to escape. There was only one way out. I would take it.

Escape to Nowhere

It had been four months since I had left the Navy. Mentally, I had gone steadily downhill. Now, my ability to concentrate and cope with life's challenges had completely disappeared. I could not go on like this any longer. I had to get away, to escape. But, where to? For what purpose? It did not matter. I just had to leave this life behind.

Monday morning, instead of reporting for work, I packed a few things and started driving to parts unknown. I had finally decided that taking my own life was the only way out. But the finality of it all! For once done, there is no turning back. I had to be sure that was what I wanted to do. I just knew I could not face another day of hell at work. I would drive and drive until I had made a final decision. I had plenty of time. Now, there was no more pressure to meet society's demands. My fate was in my own hands.

For the next two weeks, I traveled randomly throughout the South, going from one place to another with no particular purpose or destination. Some days, I would lie in bed all day, staring blankly at the television. Sometimes, I would spend all day, just lying in bed, reliving my life. What had led me to this place and time? Had I lost my mind? I was totally absorbed in myself and my own destiny. I had no thoughts of my family and the pain they would go through when they learned of my disappearance. I cared not what my employer would think. My whole life was on the line. That was all I cared about.

Meanwhile, back in Charlotte and Nashville, things were in an uproar. When I did not report for work, my employer sought to locate me. The Charlotte police got involved. An all points bulletin was put out throughout North Carolina and neighboring states. My picture was plastered across television screens. Foul play was suspected. My family in Nashville feared the worst. My mother, subject to bouts of depression herself, was distraught.

My mother's brother and a cousin on my mother's side set out for Charlotte to investigate. They both had full-time jobs but left their jobs behind for the sake of the family. My father said he was too busy to go. When my uncle and cousin arrived in Charlotte, the apartment manager let them in my apartment.

Of course, nothing was askew. No sign of a struggle. There was nothing to indicate what had happened to me. They did find a letter from Gloria. They called her and of course she was dumfounded, but could shed no light on the mystery. My uncle and brother returned to Nashville with nothing to report.

About two weeks after I "disappeared," I found myself lying in bed in Knoxville. I suppose I had returned there because it had been such an important part of my life. Even in my confused and bewildered mental state, I realized I could not roam the country forever. Something had to be done now. I could wait no longer. The next day I would solve my problem once and for all.

The next morning, I shaved for the first time in several days. I also put on the best clothes that I had brought with me. I wanted to look like a reputable citizen. Then, I went to a local gun shop. I had finally convinced myself that taking my own life was the only way to end my suffering. When I entered the store, there were several customers. The clerk was so busy with other customers that he paid no attention to me.

I finally found, on display, the weapon I had in mind, a .45 caliber handgun. I had carried such a weapon in Vietnam for a year and knew how to use it. I am not sure exactly how long I stood there staring at that weapon. It could have been a minute or ten minutes. I had no concept of time. Many scenes from my life crossed my mind. I thought of my family. I also thought of life itself. What if there is no afterlife? What if this life is all there is? I also thought of God. Life is precious. I had to hold on to it no matter what fate befell me. No, I could not kill myself. But I knew what I had to do, this time for sure. I turned and walked out of the store empty-handed.

It was still early morning. I went back to the motel, packed my things, checked out and headed for Nashville. The three hour drive to Nashville was peaceful and blissful. My mind was at rest. From now on, I would never have to "fake it" anymore.

I could be myself. I was going where I would be accepted "as is." I did not get in touch with my family when I returned to Nashville. I knew that they would learn of my fate soon enough. I drove straight to the state psychiatric hospital in Nashville. I sat at the front gate a few minutes, fearing yet yearning to go inside. Finally, I got the nerve to enter the hospital and go up to the admission desk. I knew, without a doubt, that this was where I would spend the rest of my life. There was no chance that I would ever have to "fake it" anymore. Here, they would understand. I had found my final sanctuary.

7
Psychiatric Hospital

Hopeless Souls

When I arrived at the hospital, I was admitted on a thirty-to-forty man ward that would be my home for what, I thought, would be the rest of my life. There were no individual rooms on the ward, just six-man cubicles with walls about five feet high between the cubicles. It was designed this way so that the staff could monitor the activities of the patients at all times.

Upon first meeting the other patients, I was shocked. Except for my grandmother, I had never before been around seriously mentally ill people. I had been feeling sorry for myself, my predicament and my future. I should have realized that there were people much worse off than I. Even though seriously depressed with, in my own mind, little hope for the future, at least I had a sense of reality. Many of the patients lived in "another world."

I did observe that there were a few patients on the ward that, at first, appeared "normal." I soon became aware that these were short-term patients who would only have a brief stay on the ward. Many of these short-term patients had been entered as patients primarily as a result of stopping taking their prescribed medications. Failure to take prescribed medications was a problem common to both short-term and long-term patients. When the short-term patients restarted taking the proper medication once again, they usually left the ward in a week or so, returned to society and, hopefully, began living normal lives. However, these short-term patients made up only a very small percentage of the patients on the ward. Many of the patients on the ward consisted of "hopeless souls" who would be institutionalized for the remainder of their lives. When I first entered the hospital, I considered myself to be among that group.

Most people are unfamiliar with those who have completely lost any sense of reality and live in their own world. That is because most of such people are institutionalized, hidden away from society. Society would rather pretend that they don't exist, as most citizens go about their daily lives. Only the family members of the mentally ill can know the feeling of anguish and hopelessness they feel as they watch their loved ones sink into the dark recesses of their own minds.

Most long-term patients were on strong medications to modify their behavior and keep them from "acting out." Therefore, much of the time the ward was relatively peaceful. However, one did not have to be on the ward long before the devils that plagued each patient's soul became obvious.

Had I not already been severely depressed, being exposed to these other patients might have done the trick. Being exposed to continuous erratic and disturbing behavior might have been bad for my psyche. However, as usual, I was more concerned about my ultimate fate than I was with the bizarre behavior going on around me. But being around all this did make me wonder: "Was I doomed to be just another one of the hopeless souls?"

I should say something about the staff. Almost all were black. They were in dead-end jobs, being paid little. On the day shift in particular, most lacked the education or work experience to do much better. Most were just working to pay the bills. Yet, most did their best to treat the patients humanely, if not always with understanding and sympathy. It was a thankless job for which there was no adulation or praise for a job well done.

Since most patients went to bed very early, the staff at night was much smaller than the day shift. Usually it consisted of only three persons, the woman in charge and two young assistants. The two young assistants deserve special adulation. Some of the patients were all alone in the world with only the staff to attend to their needs and comfort them. Some families, long ago having realized the hopelessness of their loved one's recovery had, in effect, abandoned them. These two young assistants were both students at Tennessee State University by day and worked at the hospital by night. Both treated each patient, no matter how ornery or unresponsive, with tender loving care and respect, as though each were a family member. I will never forget the two young men.

After I had gone to bed those first few nights, I had pondered my fate. Was there any hope for me? Would I be here for the rest of my life? Being in a place where most were "life's losers," I had surely reached the low point of my life. However, soon after I arrived at the hospital, I met my savior, the woman who lifted me from the depths of despair to some semblance of normalcy, my "Mother Teresa."

Mother Teresa

Doctor Elizabeth Vorbusch, the doctor in charge of the ward on which I was a patient, turned out to be my "Mother Teresa." Dr. Vorbusch had a thankless task. She was overburdened with the number of patients under her care. It was probably very frustrating to her that there was little she could do for most of them. Probably, her only satisfaction was in helping the short-term patients go out into the world with a fighting chance of living a normal life. I realized soon after I met Doctor Vorbusch that she thought that I was somehow different from the "hopeless souls" destined to be institutionalized for the remainder of their lives. I soon realized that she believed that I was worth saving.

It did not take but one visit with me for "Mother Teresa" to determine that depression was my problem. I am sure that having worked in the hospital for many years and seeing innumerable patients suffering from depression, the diagnosis came very easily. She immediately started me on her antidepressant of choice. I often wonder why the Navy doctors whose care I was under during my hospitalizations at two different Navy hospitals in California just two years previously had failed to diagnose me as suffering from depression. Had they made a proper diagnosis and treatment, I might have received the help I needed at that time that would have saved me from the bottomless pit of despair to which I had fallen.

Antidepressants are a "hit and miss" proposition, which helps explain why I did not receive immediate relief by the antidepressant first prescribed for me. But Dr. Vorbusch was dedicated to the proposition that I was one severely depressed patient that could be "saved." When it became obvious that a particular antidepressant was doing me little if any good, she would try another.

All the doctors at the hospital took turns spending twenty-four hour shifts so that a doctor would be immediately available in case of an emergency. Dr. Vorbusch took her turn about every sixth day. Usually, it was a quiet time for the doctor on duty. Nothing much happened while all patients were supposed to be asleep.

It soon became a ritual every time that Dr. Vorbusch had duty that she would have me come to her office after the other patients were asleep. It was usually around 10:00 P.M. when she invited me to join her in her office. While most doctors on duty chose to sleep unless some emergency came up, Dr. Vorbusch and I would talk until the wee hours of the morning. She delved into all aspects of my life seeking to find the circumstances leading me to such a severely depressed state. I held nothing back. I told her things about myself that I had never revealed to anyone else. Often, I would cry uncontrollably for a few minutes. Initially, I could tell that she thought that my recent experience in Vietnam might be the catalyst for my depression. However, after I told her about my "meltdowns" in 1963 and 1967, the innermost secrets of my dysfunctional childhood, and the fate of my grandmother, she soon realized that my problems ran much deeper and had little, if anything, to do with my service in Vietnam.

Shortly after we began our routine late night talks, Dr. Vorbusch decided that it was doing me no good to spend my entire daytime hours, day after day, in the turmoil on the ward. She thought my time would be better spent in more quiet surroundings. She asked me if I would like to work in the hospital library. I jumped at the chance. After being continuously on the ward for weeks, I sought nothing more than solitude. Soon after breakfast each day, I would go to the hospital library to spend most of the day. After a "breaking in" period, I was put completely in charge of the library function, although a staff supervisor was in an adjoining room. This might sound like a tremendous responsibility for a patient; however, it turned out to be little more than a chance for me to get off the ward, as the library experienced very little activity. Even for a patient suffering from depression, it was not much of a challenge.

I soon found that the hospital library was utilized by only a handful of patients. Many patients that did wander in merely meandered aimlessly in a daze, never stopping to read books at the available tables or bothering to check books out. One of the few patients who did actually check out books was an elderly man who was a regular every single day. He never missed a day. This gentleman, who I was told had once been a physician, checked four books out every single day. I could tell by his demeanor that he was unlikely to read one word from any of the books. But sure enough, the next day he would return the four books and check out four different ones. I surmised that as a physician he had probably been a prolific reader. In the dark recesses of his psyche, he still felt it necessary to attempt to read. Some things one may never forget even when one's ability to comprehend and reason are gone.

When I first checked myself into the hospital, I had no desire to see anyone. I was lost in the dark recesses of my own soul. However, as might be expected, my mother, having once thought her oldest son had probably perished, could not be kept away. She visited several times a week. As might be expected, my father was a "no show." I imagine he was too busy amassing his worldly treasures on earth. I asked my mother not to bring my sister and brothers to see me. I did not want them to see me in the condition that I was in.

Finally, after about three months in the hospital, Dr. Vorbusch put me on a medication that proved to be beneficial. At first, I did not notice much difference in my outlook toward the world or any change in my temperament. But gradually, I began to feel a little better each day. For the first time in a long time, not all my thoughts were negative. I am sure that Dr. Vorbusch noted a slight improvement in my demeanor. I could sense by the way she smiled at me that she thought I was on the road to recovery. Each night when I went to bed, for once, I began to feel that tomorrow would be better than the day before. I was confident that "help was on the way."

About the middle of March, after I had been on the medication that had proven effective for approximately a month, Dr. Vorbusch was so impressed with my improvement that she asked me if I would consider entering a "halfway house." A halfway house is where patients who are not sure they are quite ready to re-enter society, can live with others in a similar predicament and help ease each other's re-entry into the "real world." Displaying more self confidence than I actually felt, I replied "No. I want to go home." Dr. Vorbusch was both surprised and pleased. We agreed that I would leave the hospital within a few days. In reality, the last place I wanted to go was to my parents' home. I had too many bad memories there. But where else could I go?

I had serious misgivings about leaving the hospital. Could I survive in the real world? However, lying in bed at night I had come to the conclusion that, for better or worse, I had to get on with my life. I could not hide from the world forever. I must fight and conquer whatever demons awaited me "out there." I knew that I was not depression free but my improvement had been such that I could now, for the most part, satisfactorily focus and concentrate. So, as the staff gathered and wished me well, I took my first baby steps into the unknown. At twenty-six I was starting all over again. I hoped that my future would be better than my past.

8

Starting Over

Job Search

When I left the hospital, I moved back home with my family. I hoped it would not be for long. I had been on my own since high school. I was used to doing exactly what I wanted to do when I wanted to do it. I did not wish to live at home where my every move would be scrutinized, particularly since the events of the past few months. I wanted to find a place of my own; however, as my savings from Vietnam were practically depleted, I knew that my first priority was finding a job, and fast.

I must admit that although worldly wise since my stint in the Navy, I was very naïve about the difficulty in finding a job. I assumed that having been an honors graduate from UT and having served three years as a naval officer, I would have a "leg up" in finding a job and a career. Of course, I was wrong. Never underestimate the stigma attached to having had mental problems. A lengthy stay in a state mental hospital, considered the end of the line by most, was a career killer. I would be lucky to find any open-minded employer willing to take a chance on me.

I was very aggressive in applying for jobs. Within a week, I had arranged several job interviews in late March or early April. I was overqualified for some of the positions for which I applied. I surmised that if I could just get my foot in the door at a reputable firm or a company, I could prove myself and move up. I was very confident that finding an acceptable position would soon be in the offing.

All of my interviews proceeded along in the same manner. When reviewing my academic and work history, all of the prospective employers appeared impressed. However, everything changed when they reached the part of my resume detailing my four month stay at the state psychiatric hospital. They seemed embarrassed as they began to back paddle. All of a sudden, many obstacles to my being hired were brought up. The interviewers tried to be nice but it was apparent that they were not willing to take a chance on me. Realizing that the mental health issue was the cause for their reticence, I tried to assure them that since I had begun receiving the proper medication, I had been "normal" and saw no reason to believe I would not be so in the future. I could tell that my plea fell on deaf ears. Although all were cordial and promised to "get back with me," I knew the handwriting was on the wall. I knew that I would never hear from any of them again. I didn't.

After my first interview, I seriously considered altering my resume to "cover up" my hospital stay and somehow otherwise account for my whereabouts since being discharged from the Navy. I knew that I could not mention my short stint in the fall of 1969 with the firm in Charlotte. When contacted, they would surely "spill the beans." Would it be so unusual for a Vietnam veteran to buy a new car and "discover America" for a few months? Would that seem plausible? Finally I realized that that would not be me. I had always been brought up to tell the truth and be completely "above board" in dealing with other people. Could I now lead a life of deception? Would I have to live in constant fear of my "awful secret" coming to light? No, I could not go that route. Any employer would have to accept me "as is." I knew eventually that I would find some kind soul willing to give me a chance.

As almost a desperation measure, in addition to applying with prestigious companies, I had submitted my application to the state. It was really a "fallback" position, an option only if nothing else "panned out." After all, government employees were often thought of as slackers who work for the government only because reputable companies would not hire them. Many people, including my father, thought that if you worked for any governmental agency you were automatically a "loser."

Hope at last! A call came from Bill White, the Director of State Audit in the Tennessee Comptroller's Office. Mr. White asked me if I would like to interview with State Audit as an auditor. It was like tossing a drowning man a life vest. Instantly, I replied affirmatively. He asked me to meet him in his office at 10:00 A.M. on a Tuesday in the middle of April. I was sitting in his outer office at 9:30 A.M.. I didn't want to be late for what could be my last opportunity at a job commensurate with my education and training. So what if the job lacked prestige? At least I would get a chance to exhibit my skills. I had to put my best foot forward. I had to get this job.

Just like all the other employers that I had interviewed, Mr. White was impressed with my credentials. However, Mr. White appeared to be much more open-minded about my mental history than many of the employers with which I had interviewed. He was very empathetic with my situation. But could he take a chance on a former mental patient? He would be subject to criticism if he hired me and I later went "off the deep end." He interrupted our interview and called Hugh Bellamy, the Assistant to the Comptroller. Would Mr. Bellamy be available to meet with Mr. White and myself the next day? Mr. Bellamy said yes. At least I had a shot.

After a lengthy discussion, with many deeply penetrating questions, I apparently "passed muster" with both Mr. White and Mr. Bellamy. Both were willing to take a chance on me. To this day, I have the utmost respect for Mr. White and Mr.

Bellamy for going out on a limb for me. They would have been subject to criticism if I had failed them. It would have been easy for them to take the "safe route" and hire an auditor with "less baggage." But they chose not to play it safe. I knew that I would not fail them.

I was to start work Friday, May 1, 1970 as a junior auditor. It did not matter that the salary was substantially below what I had hoped for and what I had made when working for the CPA firm. At last, I had a chance to prove myself. Surely, I would work for the state for only a couple of years and then move on to bigger and better things. And then again, I still had dreams of law school. Even though delighted to at last have a job opportunity, there was no chance that I would have a life-long career with the state. Was there?

Since I left the hospital in March 1970, there has not been one day in my life when I was not taking some form of antidepressant. Thankfully, because, during the '70s, I was always taking one antidepressant or another or combinations thereof, I suffered no "meltdowns." But I was far from out of the woods. My belief that the medication Dr. Vorbusch had finally found for me during the latter stages of my hospitalization would be a "cure all" proved to be unrealistic. I had many periods during the '70s when my ability to function was impaired but not to the extent that I could not "persevere" and "carry on." I had thought my days of "faking it" were over. They were not.

Fortunately, during the '70s, most of my "depressive episodes" were short-lived, not as debilitating as those I had suffered before and usually went unnoticed by most of those around me. To most, I appeared a high achiever, living a successful "normal" life. Far from it. Each time I had a "mini-episode" of depression, I feared this might be "the big one." I lived with constant fear that "the other shoe would fall" and my life, a "house of cards," would come tumbling down.

High School Reunion

Sometime in April, while I remained jobless, I was notified of the tenth annual reunion of my Central High class, to be held Saturday May 2. Since it had been only nine years since graduation, I thought having a tenth annual reunion a bit bizarre. Actually, the forces that be had decided, for some reason, to have a combined reunion with both the class of 1961, my class, and the class of 1960. It did not matter to me. With my mental history and being jobless, there was no way that I was going to suffer the humiliation of being around my old classmates. Having once being a "big man on campus," everyone would ponder how I could have fallen so low.

After I found out that I was to start work with State Audit May 1st, the day before the reunion, I began having second thoughts about attending the reunion. Having lived largely a life of "faking it" and putting up a false front for so many years, I knew that I could pull off attending the reunion without disclosing anything disparaging concerning my life. I would be as evasive as possible if asked any details about my life. Yes, I would go.

I had a great time at the reunion. I was surprised at how much the boys (men) had changed since high school, while the girls (women) looked much the same. I decided that it was a combination of girls maturing so much faster than men and women making more of an effort to retain their youth. Although some of my classmates were "blowhards," trying to impress their old classmates with their success, most were just there to relive the past and, for a while, forget that life was not the fun and games we had so innocently anticipated in our youth. Surprisingly, I was not asked any questions that I could not handle. I had become adept at putting my best foot forward and avoiding inquiries into my personal life. Fortunately, to my knowledge, my mental problems were known only to myself. I wanted to keep it that way.

After greeting and reminiscing with most of my old friends, the one person that I had hoped would be there arrived, Brenda. I knew that she had married soon after high school and had two young daughters. I also had learned through the grapevine that she had been recently divorced and was "on the market" once more. She was one of the reasons that influenced my attending the reunion in the first place. We had had "crushes" on one another during our senior year when she sat directly in front of me in our senior English class. However, since I was "going steady" with Connie for most of my senior year, Brenda and I never did anything but flirt shamelessly.

Having met and reminisced with everyone else that I really cared about seeing, Brenda and I made an early exit and found ourselves in my car "making out" as if time had stood still and we were back in high school. We made a dinner date for the following night. That was just the beginning. Soon we were in a full-blown relationship. I must admit that the combination of finally landing a job and having a relationship with an attractive woman was good for my self-confidence. My self-esteem had recently reached an all-time low. I had doubted that any woman, much less an attractive, desirable one, would have any interest in me. I began to feel alive once more.

Brenda and I spent a great deal of time together that summer and early fall. She was not overly inquisitive about my recent past and I volunteered nothing. We just enjoyed being together. Actually, I had made up a plausible story to "cover myself" if anyone became too inquisitive. However, most people did not give a damn about inquiring into my past. I was just being overly sensitive and defensive. With work progressing better than expected and going with an attractive woman obviously very attracted to me, my mental health greatly improved. To make things even better, in June I moved from my parents' home to a small efficiency apartment. Never again would I have to explain why two pair of children's shoes were left in my car.

But as is usually the case, good things have to come to an end. In spite of usually being clueless in matters of love, it eventually "dawned on me" that Brenda was looking for a permanent relationship, someone to help rear her children. It soon became obvious that I was to be "it." This became abundantly clear when, out of the blue, she concocted a transparent reason why she needed me to take her to her mother's home, some eighty miles away. This was to be "meet the parent day." I was beginning to feel hemmed in.

How could I explain to her that I lived in the constant fear of yet another "meltdown" to tear my new life asunder? Who knows, I might be just one day from catastrophe. I knew that Brenda needed a good, solid, stable man who she could count on for the long term. Having had anything but a stable past, I could not promise to be that man. I also was somewhat ashamed. I was taking advantage of her sweet, loving nature, just biding my time, enjoying the relationship without a serious thought of her or her future. It was all about me. Why did I not just do the "decent" thing and set her free to find someone to share her life with and help her rear her children? Maybe, if Brenda and I had reunited five years later, things might have turned out different. But I had found that, as with my relationship years before with Randy, in matters of the heart, timing is everything. This was definitely not the right time for Brenda and me. Our relationship had to end. It did.

9
The '70s

Found My Calling

When I reported for work at State Audit on May 1, 1970, it was a very small Division of the Comptroller's Office. During the '70s, State Audit would expand astronomically, but in 1970, its function was fairly limited. The staff primarily consisted of older people who had been there for years. The staff was so small that each auditor acted independently and reported directly to the Director, Mr. White.

Even though my experience with the national CPA firm had been less than six months, it soon became apparent that State Audit did not utilize sophisticated audit techniques and procedures, such as statistical sampling, common to all national firms. It was also obvious that the small staff size limited the division's effectiveness to "putting out fires" when problems occurred anywhere in state government. Mr. White was an effective administrator, but he was limited in his capabilities by both the size of the staff and the quality of his staff. The low wages paid by the state prevented Mr. White from attracting young accounting graduates, with new ideas, to his staff. He just did the best he could with what he had.

I had many ideas about ways in which the audit function could be improved; however, knowing that I was lucky to have a job at all, for the first few months, I kept my mouth shut and did what I was told. In my case, one advantage of being a member of such a small staff, Mr. White soon became very familiar with my performance. He seemed impressed. I was soon assigned work more challenging than normally assigned inexperienced auditors. Thankfully, I did not "drop the ball." Around October, I began making subtle suggestions of how the audit function could be improved. In most cases Mr. White was receptive to my suggestions. I began to feel that I had gained acceptance and now was a full-fledged member of the organization.

Having survived a breakup with Brenda during the fall of 1970, I began to concentrate on my work. I dated only sporadically. In May, 1971, I celebrated my first year of employment with the state and was being relied on more and more by Mr. White when he needed someone for a difficult or "politically sensitive" project. However, I continued to fear that my status in the division would be compromised if anyone other than Mr. White knew of my past mental problems. I felt I would lose the confidence and respect of the other auditors. Each month, I "sneaked off" for a couple of hours to get my medication at the outpatient clinic of the psychiatric hospital. I always feared someone would see me. No one ever did. I felt my secret was safe with Mr. White.

I have not mentioned it before but while in Vietnam, like everyone who served there, I was allowed to take a week off and leave Vietnam for rest and relaxation (R & R) at a location of my choice. I chose Australia. It was nice to get away. In December 1968, I spent a week in Sydney. It was summer in Australia. The Australians, in general, loved Americans. Soon after arriving in Sydney, an Australian-American Committee sponsored a get-acquainted dance, allowing single young women to meet the American servicemen.

At the dance, I soon "hooked up" with a young woman named Patricia. A working woman, we spent all the time together that her time constraints allowed. We wined, dined and partied while I was in Sydney. By the day, I was a beach bum at Bondi Beach relaxing from the previous night. I hoped that the week would never end. But, of course, it did. I surmised that the following week she would be back at the next dance "hooking up" with yet another American.

Patricia promised to write me in Vietnam. Figuring that I was just another one of the many men she had been with, I never really expected to hear from her. I was very surprised that after I returned to Danang, she wrote quite often. I looked forward to her letters even though I never expected to see her again. I thought that she was only doing her part to bring solace to a lonely serviceman far from home. Surprisingly, we continued to correspond once I returned to "the world," although there was a lapse during the period in 1969 when I was having my "meltdown."

In May 1971 it had been over a year since I had left the hospital. I thought that, just maybe, my serious episodes of depression were behind me. It was a time when, at last, I had some confidence that I would have a bright future. Thus, I was delighted when I got a letter from Patricia stating that she was planning on taking a two-week sojourn to America. She apparently had made no specific plans. Not wishing to miss a chance of seeing Patricia again, I spared no cost and made a long distance call to her in Sydney. I convinced her that the best way to see a "slice of America" was to spend the two weeks exploring the east coast of the country with me. She accepted the offer. She left it to me to make all the plans. We would just meet at LaGuardia Airport in New York City in July and "go from there." To me, it sounded like two weeks of paradise.

My life, it seems, has been subject to many "bumps in the road," often coming when least expected. This planned trip to New England and the east coast was no exception. About a week before I was to start my drive to New York, I realized that I was in the throes of a depressive episode. I tried to tell myself that it was only a minor incident and would soon pass. However, each day, as the trip drew nearer, I felt worse. I had had three meltdowns in my life. Now each time I felt the least bit depressed I feared another meltdown. I also wondered whether or not the antidepressant that I had been taking for over a year had lost its effectiveness. I began to panic as I, at last, finally realized that this was no minor episode.

One of the effects of being depressed is that judgment goes out the window. You can't think straight and often have delusional thoughts. I feared telling the doctors at the outpatient clinic of my problem. Would they put me back in the hospital? At any rate I had agreed to meet Patricia in New York. I would not let her down. Somehow, I would get through the two weeks, come hell or high water. I would face my problem when I got back. After work one Friday I started the drive to New York. I hoped that I could "fake it" and show Patricia a good time. Would the day ever come when I would no longer have to "fake it?"

I picked Patricia up at the airport as planned. I will not bore you with the details of the trip, only that we spent time in New York City, Boston, Cape Cod, Baltimore and Washington. The trip was very trying for me, attempting to just get through each day; however, I am convinced that Patricia thoroughly enjoyed the trip. Even in my altered state, I began to wonder if she was "auditioning" for American citizenship. Usually when depressed my libido "goes south." Not so this time. I returned her affection in kind. I do not think that she ever realized that anything was wrong. But in the back of my mind was always the thought, "What happens when I return home?"

After the two weeks had passed and Patricia and I had said our good-byes, I grudgingly returned to Nashville to face my future. I had a plan to seek relief that would preclude the possibility of the outpatient clinic ever knowing anything was wrong. It was a plan born out of desperation. Because I did not know any practicing psychiatrists, I turned to an elderly family practitioner that my family had known for years. I did not let my family know of my problem. I knew I could trust the doctor's discretion. After hearing the story of my previous episodes, of which he had previously been unaware, he prescribed an antidepressant that I had never taken before. He was confident it would help. I must admit that I did not share his confidence, but what other alternative did I have? With more hope than faith, I began taking the medication.

Of course, after I returned from my trip, I had to resume work. However, for once I caught a break. My next job assignment was rather routine, something that I could do with my eyes closed. It's a good thing. Even though my thinking was very "muddled," I managed to do a credible job, all the while waiting for my new medication to "kick in." As noted before, many medications must be taken for several weeks before any material effect is noticed. Miraculously, this new medication took effect in only a few days. Soon I felt even better than when I left the hospital. I thought that I had found a "miracle drug" that would end my depression forever. I was wrong.

Shortly after my trip through the East, Mr. White decided that since he had been allowed to hire quite a few additional auditors, the era of everyone reporting to him would be over. It should also be noted that these new auditors were mostly young, right out of college. It was time to change the old ways. Although the "old salts" that had been there for years probably resented change, they would just have to learn to adjust. Mr. White created four Audit Supervisor positions. The remaining auditors were allocated into teams with each auditor reporting to a designated supervisor. There was probably some resentment at my being chosen as one of the supervisors since I had been "on board" such a short time. Nevertheless, the new organizational structure was sound and remained intact long after Mr. White was no longer Director.

In addition to being responsible for auditing various state departments and institutions, on several occasions I was assigned to investigate specific instances of alleged fraud within the state. I usually accompanied the Comptroller's legal counsel. I was gratified that Mr. White had enough confidence in my abilities to trust me with such important and sensitive assignments. I must admit to a great deal of frustration in that the investigations sometimes seemed futile. We often confirmed fraudulent conduct by specific state employees or those dealing with the state, sometimes amounting to considerable sums. After fraudulent activity was discovered, the result usually only consisted of the person repaying the state for the amount stolen. Local District Attorneys, the only ones with authority to prosecute, usually refused to pursue cases involving theft from the state. The general attitude was that the state had so much money that stealing from the state was no big deal. As an idealist, I was deeply offended.

Sometime in late 1972 or early 1973, Mr. White accepted a position in another division of the comptroller's Office. Frazier Solomon, who had been Assistant Director of State Audit, assumed the position of Director. Mr. Solomon did not make any significant changes during his short tenure. He left for employment in the private sector in a little over a year. Following Mr. Solomon came Frank Greathouse, a tempestuous man, if there ever was one. But that is another story for a later chapter.

Throughout the '70s, I took many different medications or combinations thereof. Each time, I hoped "this was it." For sure, this would be the end of my depressive episodes. It was not to be. Although, after the episode in 1971, I regained my senses and put myself under the care of a private psychiatrist, each new medication seemed to have a "shelf-life" in my body, eventually losing its effectiveness. A new round of different antidepressants would ensue. To this day, I have never had a single moment when I was not on one antidepressant or another. Because of the medications, my depressive episodes in the '70s, although they often came at inopportune times, were usually short-lived and not as severe as some had been in the past. Only rarely during this period did I completely "lose it" and then only for short periods. Also, thank God, there were no "meltdowns" in the '70s. I came to believe those days were over. In the '80s, I would find out differently.

Looking for Love

After I stopping seeing Brenda in October 1970, for the next year I dated very little, instead, concentrating on my professional career. Of course, an exception was my two-week excursion through New England and the accompanying episode of depression in July 1971. Beginning in the fall of 1971, being twenty-eight years of age, I begin to think seriously about dating again and realized that I should use more discretion in whom I dated, concentrating more on women of substance. The time for dating just to have a good time was over. I should think seriously about meeting someone with whom I could have a future. Considering my mental history, I knew I needed a woman who would be a "rock of Gibraltar," someone very stable emotionally and mentally. The last thing I needed was someone with the fragile psyche like mine.

In 1971 and 1972, I had a few dates, but none worth mentioning. By the fall of 1972, I had something else to occupy both my mind and time, law school. I had always had a fascination with the law. I had always, in my saner moments, dreamed of going to law school. In January 1971, I had taken the Law School Admission Test (LSAT). I had scored extremely high. Had I not had all my mental and emotional baggage, my LSAT score might have been high enough to qualify for admission to a top-notch law school. But that was wishful thinking. Any reputable law school would engage in a background check that would doom my chances. I had only one hope. Since I had graduated with honors from the University of Tennessee, I thought I might have a chance at being admitted to the UT law school. I applied and was immediately accepted for admission in the fall of 1972.

My elation at being accepted was short-lived. I soon began to have second thoughts. I could expect no financial help from my family. I had no savings to speak of. Even though I qualified for veterans' benefits, three years of law school would still put me heavily in debt. Would it be worth living as a pauper for three years? Also, what were the chances of my being depression free for three years, or for that matter, thereafter? If my mental history was any indication, a depression-free future was highly unlikely. Attending UT Law School was out of the question.

But hope springs eternal. I soon found a way to "have my cake and eat it too." Even though not as prestigious as most law schools, in Nashville there was a law school which held classes at night for people who had daytime jobs. The YMCA Night Law School (later renamed the Nashville School of Law), had produced many graduates who had later earned acclaim in the legal profession. Of course working by day at a full-time job and spending nights either in school or studying would be a grueling ordeal. I felt certain that I could meet the challenge. I applied and was quickly admitted. I started classes in the fall of 1972.

Often relationships come when you least expect them, when you have stopped searching for them. Such was the case for me. In the fall of 1972, I threw myself "head over heels" into both my work and law school. I really did not have much time for anything else. I did note that State Audit had hired several new auditors, among them a young woman named Judy, whom I thought attractive. After I had gotten "settled in" in law school, I asked Judy out. She accepted. That was a major turning point in my life. I soon was trying to juggle seeing Judy, working and law school. I saw Judy mainly on weekends. Law school and studying occupied my weeknight hours. Judy was very understanding.

Days turned into weeks, weeks into months. Soon it was May 1973. Judy and I had been seeing each other exclusively for eight months. I tried to find flaws in Judy. I could find none. She was intelligent, a "must" for a potential life partner. She was not only of the highest character but she was even tempered and got along well with everyone. Having seen my mother "nag" my father incessantly (often he deserved it), most importantly, Judy never gave me a "hard time" about anything. Even more importantly, I thought Judy, being so emotionally stable, was the "Rock of Gibraltar" for which I had long been searching. With Judy there was a "comfort zone" that had eluded me in my past relationships.

Most people think of women with regard to their being aware of their "biological clock ticking." Although not quite comparable, there comes a time in most men's lives when they tire of "chasing the future" and decide instead, to make it happen. Nearing thirty, I felt that that time had come for me. I was ready to settle down and start a family. Judy was a woman that was as perfect as any woman could be. I admired and respected her. I held her in high esteem. I could never find a finer woman. I thought that would be enough to sustain a lifelong relationship. A few years later, to my dismay, I found it wasn't.

Starting a Family

Judy and I were married in August 1973. After a wedding trip to Miami, we settled into an apartment in the Southeast section of Nashville, near the airport. The choice of location was not random. Prior to our marriage, Judy left State Audit and obtained a position as Internal Auditor at Middle Tennessee State University in Murfreesboro, some thirty miles southeast of Nashville. With an interstate highway leading to Murfreesboro at our doorstep, Judy could probably arrive at her work before I could reach mine in traffic-snarled downtown Nashville.

Soon after our marriage, I began my second year of law school at night. Much of my time the next three years would be devoted to my studies. Thus, our social life consisted primarily of a movie and dinner on Saturday night. This became a ritualized routine throughout the three remaining years in law school. An exception to this routine came when I contacted several of my high school friends who I knew liked to play bridge. We soon formed a "bridge club," which continued once a month bridge sessions for several years.

Like most law school students, I soon found myself in a study group which met regularly to compare notes of previous classes and discuss pertinent cases. The study group was small, consisting only of Bobby Ellis, a compatriot of mine in State Audit, Dent Morris, an early morning "disc jockey" on a local radio station and me. The regular study group sessions endured for the entire three years we had remaining on our legal studies and put a serious dent into all of our social lives. It was not difficult for me to become obsessed with the study of law. I found it fascinating. The only negative thought I had was whether or not it would ever be possible for me to put my study of law into practice. Susceptible to periodic depressive episodes, dare I take a chance of practicing law? Auditing, which I enjoyed and at which I was proficient, afforded a much more secure future. Oh well, I would save that decision for another day.

Even though I was still in denial that I might possibly be susceptible to depressive episodes for the rest of my life and that my gene pool, with regard to mental issues, might be a disaster area, in January 1974, Judy and I decided to attempt to start a family. Success came more rapidly than anticipated. In February, Judy announced that she was pregnant. We immediately decided that an apartment was no place to rear a child. Even though both being state employees and with little financial resources, we decided that we could afford a modest "starter home." We found one in the Tusculum area of south Nashville. At the time law school was in summer recess and when Judy was six months pregnant, we moved into our new home in August 1974.

On Monday, November 18, 1974, our first daughter, Shannon, was born at 9:10 P.M. However, it was a little after 10:00 P.M. before I was first able to see my new daughter, That night, as I stood watching my new daughter, although still in shock, yet proud, who should appear but my "study group" buddies, Bobby and Dent. Noting my absence from our Monday night law class and knowing Judy's due date was approaching, they correctly assumed the obvious and came straight to the hospital after class. As a result of their visit, Shannon had the distinction of having her birth widely heralded throughout the middle Tennessee region Tuesday morning via Dent Morris on his morning DJ radio show.

Before Judy and I married, I was candid with her about my history of depression. In spite of the risk of my incurring future mental problems, Judy, by a leap of faith, agreed to marry me anyway. However, after we married, I tried my best to conceal any depressive episodes I might have from her. I wanted both to spare her pain and to not give her any reason to question the wisdom in having chosen me as a mate. Concealing any mental episodes that I experienced was not difficult. At night, when home, life was always "laid back." I usually mellowed out, reading or watching television, two activities easy to "fake" when unable to focus or concentrate. I don't think Judy ever realized the struggles that I went through when the "mini depressive periods" occurred. For that I was thankful.

Law school and work were another matter, both difficult to "muddle through" when mentally distressed. The trials I experienced at work will be addressed in the next chapter. As for law school, I devised a way to keep from falling behind or being forced to withdraw from school when not mentally "with it." I sat on the front row of each class, directly in front of the teachers. I taped every single lecture. When unable to concentrate or think clearly while in class, the tapes saved the day. When I finally escaped the throes of a depressive episode, I could extensively review the tapes. No one, in my law school class, including Bobby and Dent, ever realized that I suffered from depression.

As we all know, when one is busy, the time flies. I watched Shannon grow from a baby in November 1974 to a mischievous toddler during the less than two years from her birth until I finished law school in June 1976. My perseverance and relentless dedication to pursuing the law paid off. I am proud to say that I graduated third out of a class of eighty-three.

Next, came the Bar Examination in July. That summer was fraught with many distractions. Immediately prior to the Bar Exam came the Bicentennial celebration, marking two hundred years of American independence with numerous commemorating festivities. The political arena was also heating up, with both the Democratic and Republican conventions to follow later that summer. In addition, there was all the hoopla surrounding the upcoming summer Olympics. July 1976 was not a good time to need to concentrate on taking any important examination

Yet, I passed the Bar Exam. Shortly, I was sworn in with the authority to practice law. At last, the day came that I had been both fondly awaiting yet dreading, when I could no longer put off choosing my future. Would it be auditing or the law? I loved the law, but I could not deny that I had a keen eye for auditing. Even though it had been over six years since my last complete "meltdown," I definitely had not been a picture of mental health in the intervening years.

The advantage of choosing the law would be the chance to "do good," to right the wrongs of society. At least, that is what, as an idealist, I believed with a passion. But the more practical Bob realized that although the opportunities for "doing good" were substantial, the risks were astronomical. What if I had another "meltdown" lasting weeks, if not months? Not only would my law practice be destroyed, with many clients left "holding the bag," my family would suffer financial ruin. To achieve great things in life, one often has to incur great risks. I would never achieve great things. I was not willing to put my future and my family at risk. I would play it safe. I would stay in the "safe arms" of the state. Subsequent events proved that decision the correct call.

Devil or Angel

In late 1973 or early 1974, there was a new sheriff in town. Frank Greathouse became the Director of State Audit. Mr. Greathouse was a very intelligent man who had a vision for State Audit far surpassing that of his predecessors. He wanted to make State Audit a force to be reckoned with in state government. He was very uncompromising in his approach. It was his way or the highway. In order to accomplish his goals, in the '70s, the size of the staff grew like "topsy."

Mr. Greathouse was a gruff, no-nonsense man who was sure of himself. Once he made a decision, hell or high water could not change his mind. He was feared, yet respected, by State Audit staff. He was so sure of himself and demanding that, later, I came to believe that even his boss, the Comptroller William Snodgrass, felt somewhat intimidated in his presence.

Mr. Greathouse had not been Director long before Tennessee, and in fact all states, had to "come to grips" with the awesome task of transferring certain welfare programs from the states to the federal government. Millions of dollars were at stake as the states and the feds haggled over this monstrous and very complicated issue. The states decided to form a committee to "look into the situation" and report back to all the states on the correct approach to take in dealing with the federal government. Prominent people were chosen to be members of this committee and represent the states. Mr. Greathouse, through the years, had gained quite a reputation among influential financial representatives throughout the country. Thus, Mr. Greathouse was selected to be a member of the committee.

The meetings of the committee were to be held at the massive Social Security complex in Baltimore. The work of the committee being very tedious and the committee in fact "plowing new ground," it took well over a year before the issue was resolved. The committee needed a staff to do the "grunt work." Mr. Greathouse volunteered me to serve as a member of the staff. The committee staff consisted of three persons, junior financial persons from Wisconsin and New York and me. The committee met almost monthly for over a year. On almost every occasion, I would accompany Mr. Greathouse to Baltimore. On a couple of occasions, when Mr. Greathouse was unable to make the trip, he would send me alone, always instructing me on his views and how to vote on any contentious issues. On one such occasion, when I was to represent Mr. Greathouse in Baltimore, something happened that would forever change my relationship with Mr. Greathouse and change my opinion of what I thought was a self-centered, unfeeling man.

In the early meetings of the committee, I had once represented Mr. Greathouse in Baltimore. He seemed pleased at the way I had handled the situation. Thus. it was probably without trepidation on his part that one Tuesday in early 1975 he informed me that, due to a conflict in his schedule, I would have to, once again, represent him at the committee meeting the following Monday. At the time it seemed, to me, like no big deal. I felt that once again I would increase my standing in his sight by effectively "carrying the ball."

By Thursday, I realized that I was entering into a depressive episode. I always feared the worst when a depressive episode began, fearing this might be "the big one." However, on most prior occasions, my fears had been unfounded. I had always managed to somehow "muddle through" and "get by." However, by Saturday, I realized this was no "mini episode." I could not think rationally. My mind was a "mess," completely unable to function.

What was I to do? Knowing Mr. Greathouse's "hard nosed" persona, I felt helpless. I just had to go to Baltimore, but knew that if I did, I would prove to be an embarrassment to Mr. Greathouse and myself. Several times Saturday afternoon, I stared at myself in the mirror and tried to convince myself that I could "do it." But, in my heart, I knew that I couldn't. I had no choice but to throw myself on Mr. Greathouse's mercy. My career in State Audit would be over. Yet, I knew what I had to do. That night, I called Mr. Greathouse and, trying to hold back both the tears and my sense of desperation, asked him if I could come over and talk to him. He agreed.

On the drive to his home, I tried to concoct some plausible reason why I could not represent him in Baltimore. Whatever story that I finally came up with was to no avail. When he opened the door, I caved in, weeping uncontrollably. Before I knew it, I was baring my soul to him, telling him everything about my mental history, of which he knew nothing. I also told him of my current inability to effectively function. I just could not possibly represent him in Baltimore. I would be an embarrassment to both him and myself.

The unforgiving nature that he had always displayed at work was, amazingly, replaced by a kind, understanding and compassionate man. As he hugged me he said, "Don't worry Bob. I will get someone else to go to Baltimore. Just take a few days off until you are feeling better." When I left his home that night, in spite of the emotional trauma that I was experiencing, I felt like I would somehow survive. I had, at last, found the father I never had.

Knowing the "other side" of Mr. Greathouse and that he was now cognizant of my "condition," I felt that somehow, barring another complete "meltdown," I could somehow survive in State Audit. In fact, I was to work in State Audit for another seven years. Gratefully, Mr. Greathouse never brought up my "Saturday night confession" again. Yet, it changed the nature of our relationship. Looking back, some thirty years later, I now realize that, thereafter, he was very protective of me. He still called me to task when I did something that did not suit him. He gave me no slack with regard to my work. However, he no longer "ranted and raved" at me, like I so often heard him do when addressing others. With his knowledge of my tender psyche, he always discussed my transgressions in a calm, cool manner.

He also seemed to instinctively realize when I was "not quite myself" suffering yet another "mini episode." He never gave me a difficult assignment when he realized I was not on "top of my game." Yet, when he realized that I was "normal," he trusted me in some of the most trying situations. It did not escape his attention that in spite of my mental instability, I was an excellent auditor and investigator.

Test of Character

As an audit Supervisor in the Division of State Audit of the state Comptroller's Office from 1971 until the summer of 1977, I had never taken political considerations into account in my audits or investigations. No one, including the Director of State Audit or the Comptroller had ever attempted to influence me in any manner with regard to such matters. In the summer of 1977, all that changed. I was given an assignment that not only would be front page news for months but would bring into question my own ethical behavior, my own character and that of my superiors. It was a defining period in my life.

The 1970s were a volatile period in Tennessee's political history. In 1975, Ray Blanton assumed the office of Governor. He followed Winfield Dunn who in 1970 had become the first Republican governor in decades. The political arena was very contentious. During Governor Blanton's term, he had appointed Marie Ragghianti, a former extradition officer, as Chairman of the State Board of Pardons and Paroles. On August 3, 1977, Governor Blanton summarily fired Ms. Ragghianti.

Governor Blanton claimed that the firing of Ms. Ragghianti resulted from her missing board meetings and the submission of alleged fraudulent travel claims to the state for reimbursement. I soon found out that the audit work uncovering Ms. Ragghianti's misdeeds had been performed by the Department of Corrections' Internal Auditor. This gave me pause. Why would the governor take such an important action and put his reputation on the line based on this man's audit work? Since he joined the Department of Corrections, I had had many dealings with him. I can only say that I would not rest my reputation on any audit work performed by him.

After Ms. Ragghianti's removal as Chairman of the State Board of Pardons and Paroles, she immediately filed suit against the state. Her attorney was Fred Thompson, who had gained fame as minority counsel for the Senate Watergate Committee during the investigation preceding President Nixon's resignation as president. In 1977, Mr. Thompson was practicing law in the middle Tennessee area. He would later serve as a Senator from Tennessee and, as of this writing, is a candidate for the Republican nomination for president in 2008.

The Comptroller, in Tennessee, is elected by the state legislature and, in theory at least, is independent of the executive branch headed by the governor. Thus, the Comptroller, as an independent party, was called upon to investigate the charges against Ms. Ragghianti. Mr. Snodgrass, the Comptroller, called upon Mr. Greathouse, the Director of State Audit to assign someone to audit Ms. Ragghianti's travel claims to determine whether or not the travel claims were indeed fraudulent. Because for several years, I had had the responsibility of auditing the Department of Corrections and was familiar with the department's financial matters, I was given the assignment of heading up the audit of Ms. Ragghianti's travel claims.

Being somewhat naïve, I assumed that auditing Ms. Ragghianti's travel claims would be a routine matter. Both Judy, the auditor whom I had assigned to do the detail work, and I had a great deal of experience in such matters. I was wrong about this case being routine. This would not be a routine audit but would result in a full-blown investigation.

In the course of our investigation, Mr. Greathouse and I met several times with Ms. Ragghianti and Mr. Thompson. One of the charges against Ms. Ragghianti was that she had missed many meetings of the Board of Pardons and Paroles, for which she had been reimbursed. Ms. Ragghianti admitted that she had missed these meetings. But then came the surprise. She stated that because hardened criminals whom she thought deserved the lengthy sentences that they had received were routinely coming before the Board for early release, she suspected someone "in the system" was receiving payments for these early releases. When missing a meeting, she claimed that she had been traveling throughout the state talking with district attorneys and judges, trying to ascertain their opinion on these early releases and the reasons therefore. She also asserted that the actual reason for her firing was the objections she had raised with the governor's office over some of these early releases and had nothing to do with her travel claims.

My first responsibility was to examine Ms. Ragghianti's travel claims for evidence such claims had been fraudulently submitted for reimbursement. My assistant and I examined Ms. Ragghianti's travel claims with a fine tooth comb. We tediously prepared a set of work papers to document our work. Our examination of the travel claims revealed that, in fact, Ms. Ragghianti and her Administrative Assistant, who had actually prepared the travel claims for Ms. Ragghianti's signature, had been guilty of sloppy record keeping.

However, in my prior examinations of travel claims of other high ranking executives in the state, I had, found other instances of sloppy record keeping. Executives often rely on others to complete their travel claims. I had never heard of a high level government employee being fired for such a transgression. In my opinion, sloppy record keeping aside, the key issue was: "Had Ms. Ragghianti been paid for expenses she had not incurred in her duties as Board Chairman.?" That was my mindset as the examination moved forward.

One key issue that had been raised by the Governor involved Ms. Ragghianti's absence from board hearings. The Governor's contention was that she was paid for board hearings which she had not attended. With regard to this issue, one day Mr. Greathouse called me into his office and informed me that I, along with State Audit legal counsel, was to go to the state prison in Nashville and interview prisoners who had appeared before the board meetings in question. We were to ask if Ms. Ragghianti had been present at these board meetings.

I could not believe what I was hearing. Had not Ms. Ragghianti already admitted to missing some of the board meetings? Were we to rely on the credibility of hardened criminals, who since they remained in prison, had been turned down for parole? Mr. Greathouse said nothing as I recounted all the reasons that this was a bad idea. After I had argued my case, he simply said "Bob, we have no choice. Just do it." I realized this decision had come from "the top."

The legal counsel and I did, in fact, go to the state prison and interviewed several inmates. Naturally, the inmates were suspicious of our motives. Just why were we there? As the whole event quickly turned into a "circus," I wondered that myself. In any event, we left the prison knowing no more than when we had arrived at the prison.

The next day I was in Mr. Greathouse's outer office, when in came Mr. Thompson. He stormed past me and burst into Mr. Greathouse's office. He was irate. At the top of his voice, he began lambasting Mr. Greathouse. "What were you thinking sending your people to interview criminals?" Mr. Greathouse, normally one who rises to meet a challenge, muttered something so low it was inaudible to me. I decided it was time for me to "get out of Dodge." Not wanting to be drawn into this confrontation, I "beelined" down the hall to my office.

The question remained, "Where was Ms. Ragghianti when she was not in board meetings?" She claimed to be doing other things in conjunction with board business. Was she? During the course of our investigation, we interviewed everyone we could reasonably expect to shed light on the subject. I personally telephoned every attorney general and judge that Ms. Ragghianti claimed to have visited in her own investigation of the early release of hardened criminals. Every district attorney and judge that I spoke to confirmed that she was with them on the dates specified although, not surprisingly, most were reluctant to reveal the subject matter discussed.

It was time to prepare an audit report. I was assigned the task of preparing a draft report for review by Mr. Greathouse and Mr. Snodgrass. Of course, Mr. Snodgrass would make the final decision of what to include in the report. In the early summer of 1978, I drafted an audit report and gave it to Mr. Greathouse. He scheduled a meeting with Mr. Snodgrass for the three of us to go over the draft report to determine the final product.

I was convinced that Ms. Ragghianti had not intentionally submitted fraudulent travel claims. I must admit that I was, in fact, sympathetic to her cause. Nevertheless, the draft report I submitted to Mr. Greathouse contained only the facts we had discovered during the many months of the audit and investigation. I stated no opinion, only facts. I felt that since Mr. Snodgrass's name would be on the report, it was up to him to decide what was in the report and draw any conclusions that he felt supported by the facts.

When Mr. Greathouse, Mr. Snodgrass and I met to review the draft report, I was surprised at the limited number of changes Mr. Snodgrass wished to make. The changes were mostly cosmetic, rewording sentences and the like. However, Mr. Snodgrass decided, on his own, to add the following sentence: "Ms. Ragghianti was less than diligent in the performance of her duties." I was stunned. I did not feel that sentence was justified by the facts uncovered in the investigation. I also felt that statement inconsistent with the rest of the report I had spent so much time drafting. Maybe I should have spoken up. Yet, I sat there and said nothing. I rationalized that it was Mr. Snodgrass's report and he could say anything he pleased. He would have to defend that sentence, not me. Or so I thought.

As I later found out from Mr. Greathouse, when Mr. Thompson received a copy of the draft report, he exploded. He was soon on the phone with Mr. Snodgrass. Mr. Greathouse was in Mr. Snodgrass's office when Mr. Thompson called. Mr. Thompson, apparently, "read the riot act" to Mr. Snodgrass for having the audacity to say that Ms. Ragghianti was less than diligent in performing her duties. According to Mr. Greathouse, that sentence was the only objection Mr. Thompson had with the report. However, Mr. Snodgrass was furious.

That day, I was reviewing audit work papers in the Department of Mental Health, not knowing of the brewing storm. I received a call from Mr. Snodgrass. He was livid. "What do you mean saying in the report that Marie Ragghianti was less than diligent in performing her duties?" Without thinking of the possible consequences, I shouted back "I didn't put that in the report. You did." There was silence for a few seconds, then the click of the phone. Mr. Greathouse later told me, "I thought the boss was going to fire you on the spot."

A final report was never released. Perhaps Mr. Snodgrass was happy that fate intervened and he could avoid taking a stand on the firing. The trial regarding Ms. Ragghianti's claim against the state was on the docket for July 1978. Mr. Thompson already knew where Mr. Snodgrass stood on the issue of the firing. That was obvious. He probably wrongly thought that Mr. Greathouse was also "in the Governor's pocket." Instead, surprisingly, Mr. Thompson issued a subpoena in early July to take my deposition. I could only surmise that during the many discussions Mr. Thompson and Ms. Ragghianti had had with Mr. Greathouse and me, Mr. Thompson had decided that I might be the only one involved in the investigation by the Comptroller's Office that did not have a political agenda.

During the course of the extensive investigation, Mr. Greathouse and I had met with Mr. Snodgrass several times, in Mr. Snodgrass's office, to discuss the case. In these discussions, Mr. Snodgrass made no attempt to influence my audit and investigation; however, it was patently clear from the discussions that Mr. Snodgrass hoped that the actions of the Governor, a fellow Democrat, would prove justified. I was very tight-lipped during these discussions, stating the facts uncovered but not stating my overall opinion. With each meeting, I felt more uncomfortable, as I was gradually reaching the conclusion that the firing was political in nature, far from the conclusion Mr. Snodgrass hoped I would reach.

When I received the subpoena to have my deposition taken by Mr. Thompson, I realized that it was inevitable that I would soon be considered a traitor by Mr. Snodgrass. But there was no way out. I had to appear for the deposition and I had to be truthful. I had expected the deposition to be rather informal, with perhaps, just myself, Mr. Thompson and a stenographer present. I was shocked when I arrived for the deposition and found a room full of people. The only person I recognized, except Mr. Thompson, was a member of the state Attorney General's Office, whose name I cannot recall. I was so nervous that I don't recall exactly what I said during the deposition, but it must have pleased Mr. Thompson. Apparently, it pleased hardly anyone else.

Immediately after the deposition, I went to Mr. Greathouse's office to discuss my deposition with him. Mr. Greathouse was a man with whom I felt close kinship and whom I felt understood my predicament. Just as I entered Mr. Greathouse's office he received a telephone call. It was from the Assistant Attorney General who had attended the deposition. Without telling the caller that I was in the room, Mr. Greathouse put the call on the speaker phone. We both just listened as the Assistant Attorney General lambasted my testimony. Did Mr. Greathouse know that he had a traitor in his employ? During the time the assistant went on and on with his ranting, Mr. Greathouse expressed no opinion. He just listened. After the call was over, Mr. Greathouse looked over at me and said, "Bob, I am proud of you, but the boss won't be." I could hold back my emotions no longer. I broke down and cried. I knew that I had one person in my corner. But what would Mr. Snodgrass do?

I thought the worst was over. It wasn't. The next day, Mr. Thomson subpoenaed me as his witness for the trial that would come in about two weeks. I spent the following two weeks in agony. I had visions of my testimony being splashed across the news media. Could I survive in the Comptroller's Office? Would I have to find a new job? With my mental history and the notoriety that would surely come after my testimony, would any employer have me? Would any employer want a person in their employ who had shown disloyalty to their previous boss? To me, my future appeared bleak.

The trial took several days. Mr. Thompson's office informed me of the day I was to report to the courthouse. On the appointed day, I took my huge box of work papers and met Mr. Thompson at the courthouse. He told me to wait outside the courtroom until I was called. That was the longest day of my life. Finally, about 3:00 P.M., Mr. Thompson exited the courtroom and smiling looked down at me and said, "Bob, I have this case won. I won't need your testimony."

I felt like the weight of the world had been lifted from my shoulders. Mr. Thompson was right. He did have this case won. The jury found that Governor Blanton had fired Ms. Ragghianti "arbitrarily and capriciously," ordered her reinstatement and awarded her $38,000 in back pay. The truth had won out. For some reason, Mr. Snodgrass chose not to fire me. Perhaps the reason for firing me would be too obvious. Or perhaps he was afraid I knew too much.

But that is not the end of the story. In January 1979, something happened to vindicate Ms. Ragghianti's belief that the system for granting clemency, pardons and paroles to state prisoners was corrupt. Because I had believed in Ms. Ragghianti, I also felt vindicated.

On January 15, 1979, Governor Blanton announced that he had granted clemency to fifty-two inmates. Soon thereafter, the U.S. Attorney, himself a Democrat, called Lamar Alexander, the recently elected Republican governor, and informed him that Governor Blanton was preparing papers to free yet another eighteen prisoners before he left office. Of these eighteen, some were targets of a grand jury investigation into corruption in Tennessee's corrections system. After a hurried series of meetings between Mr. Alexander and top legislative leaders, many of whom were Democrats, it was decided to swear in Mr. Alexander early to prevent the release of even more prisoners. Mr. Alexander was sworn in three days before his planned inauguration. All concerned, even the Democrats, felt relieved that Governor Blanton could do no further damage.

It was never proven that Governor Blanton had profited from the early release of prisoners. However, two Blanton aides were eventually convicted of selling pardons. As for Governor Blanton himself, he was later convicted for selling a liquor license. He served not quite two years in a federal prison for this offense.

Thereafter, I was given the cold shoulder by Mr. Snodgrass whenever we met. For many years after I left the Comptroller's Office, when Mr. Snodgrass and I met on the street, he would turn his head and pretend not to notice me. At any rate, I had learned the political facts of life. I was an innocent no more.

The Marie Ragghianti case left me with a sour taste in my mouth. I had once practically worshipped Mr. Snodgrass. He had been Comptroller for many years when I was hired in 1970. Everyone thought he was a "straight arrow," above politics. To this day he is admired by practically everyone. There is a large state office building in downtown Nashville bearing his name. However, I thought Mr. Snodgrass had buried his head in the sand and defended Governor Blanton's firing of Ms. Ragghianti long after it was obvious to everyone else involved in the investigation that firing Ms. Ragghianti had been an attempt to cover up corruption at the highest levels of the government. Others may continue to defend and praise him. I will always believe that he abandoned his principles for political expediency.

I knew that I did not wish to work any longer than I had to for a man I no longer respected. When you find that a boss you once idolized has "feet of clay," it is time to move on. But I was not going to quit until I found another job equally as good. They were not going to get rid of me that easy. Having so much time invested with the state, I knew my future lay in state government. I began to explore other job opportunities within the state system. However, I knew that comparable positions within state government were few and far between and that it might take a long time to obtain such a position. I would just have to bide my time. My many bouts with depression had proven me to be a survivor. I would survive this too.

The Good Life

It was almost a year between the time Governor Blanton fired Marie Ragghianti and she won her redemption in the July 1978 trial. During that time, much had happened in my personal life. Importantly, I had finally put my desire to practice law to rest. Realizing that a "meltdown" was always a possibility given my mental history, I could not take the chance of destroying my professional image, my financial security and my family's future. I would make employment by the state my career choice, the state being a "safe haven" and more forgiving of employee's deficiencies than the "dog eat dog" mentality of the legal profession.

On November 23, 1977, our second daughter was born. Judy and I named her Melanie after the Olivia DeHaviland character in *Gone with the Wind*. Judy and I still resided on Ocala Court in the Tusculum section of south Nashville, but the birth of Melanie served as a wake up call. The neighborhood in which we resided was in a period of transition. Many of the families who had resided there when we moved into this, our first home, in 1974 and with whom we had felt comfortable, had long since moved on and been replaced by neighbors that gave us pause. The children of the new families tended to be unruly, causing havoc in the neighborhood. Their favorite pastime appeared to be firing bottle rockets at anything that moved. In short, the neighborhood appeared to be "heading south." Also, there was the issue of where our young daughters would attend school when they came of age. The schools to which our daughters would be assigned, had we chosen to continue to reside on Ocala Court, had at best a mediocre reputation. Yes, everything considered, it was time to move on.

Although it would stretch our budget to the limit, we began looking at homes for sale in the Brentwood area of Williamson County, a suburb of Nashville, well within commuting distance of work for both of us and which was known to have an excellent school system. It did not take us long to find the home of our dreams, a large Tudor-style home at that time under construction on Maryland Lane in Brentwood. The fact that construction would not be completed until April 1978 was of no concern. Our oldest daughter, Shannon, was only three and would not be old enough to enter the school system anytime soon. Judy and I put down several thousand dollars "earnest money" to secure the purchase. Everything was set. Could anything go wrong?

I failed to take into account my unpredictable predilection to mental madness. Although I had had many "mini depressive episodes" since my marriage to Judy, I had never had "the big one." Although Judy was aware of my mental history when she married me, I had been successful in hiding these "mini episodes" occurring during our marriage from Judy. I saw no point in causing her concern. It was a cross that I would have to bear alone. However, shortly after depositing the earnest money on our prospective new home, I had a mental episode so severe that I could not hide it from Judy. I felt as though a complete "meltdown" was imminent. I panicked. I begged Judy to agree to forfeit our earnest money and renege on the contract. I knew we could survive on Judy's salary alone if only we remained on Ocala Court. Judy, as usual, was the "Rock of Gibraltar" I had known her to be when I married her, refusing to listen to my irrational pleadings. She insisted that we would not renege on the contract. We would move to Maryland Lane come hell or high water.

I was soon thankful to be married to such a strong-willed woman. The depressive episode, though severe and frightening, causing me as usual to foresee disaster, was as short-lived as it was severe. I soon returned to my "normal self" and looked forward to our new life on Maryland Lane. I was also thankful for the timing of the episode. It occurred during the time period in which we were making headway into the investigation regarding the firing of Marie Ragghianti. However, fortunately, during the few days of my desperation and irrational thinking, there had been a lull in the investigation. Judy was the only one that realized how close I had come to completely "losing it."

In April 1978, we moved to Maryland Lane as planned. For the next two years, we lived what appeared to everyone to be an idyllic existence. Unlike my years in law school, we had an active social life. We had lots of friends. Our bridge group continued to meet regularly. In addition, I had regularly scheduled poker games with several of my friends. Judy and I went out to dinner and a movie almost every Friday and Saturday night, hiring neighborhood teenagers to baby-sit Shannon and Melanie. Life was perfect, or was it?

I was content with my life, but I was not really happy. Did I expect too much of life, or had my years of fighting depression taken its toll? Maybe I was having the oft mentioned "mid-life crisis." I had married Judy because I knew she would be the stable influence in my life that I needed. I also knew she would be an exemplary wife and mother. Judy had proved to be a good choice on all counts. Was that enough or should there be more?

10
Life Comes Unglued

Feet of Clay

I had always thought of myself as a good person. My grandfather had instilled in me the necessity for always doing "what's right." Of course, during the many periods I had suffered depression in silence, the many "mini depressive episodes" and during the "meltdowns," my behavior sometimes had been bizarre. Yet, I cannot recall any time during those trying times that I had deliberately harmed anyone. My life was about to change. I had led my life pleasing others and trying to live up to their expectations. I was about to take charge of my own life. In April 1980, after trying unsuccessfully to rationalize what I was about to do, I did something that, even in my own mind, I could not justify. How can one defend the indefensible? I began seeing another woman.

Many men bask in the glow of an illicit relationship, having their cake and eating it too. I was not made that way. I could not cast aside all the values that I had carried with me all my life. In fact, I was miserable, consumed with guilt. How could I do this to such a wonderful wife and helpmate? I could not look at my wife without feeling shame. I knew my illicit relationship could not go undetected forever. I kept waiting for a confrontation. Maybe that is what I deserved. Perhaps the years of just trying to survive in this frightful world had engendered in me a need to self-destruct. Maybe I did not deserve to be happy. Like the moth, I was inexorably drawn to the flame, even if it meant my own destruction.

My affair continued throughout the summer and into the fall. Ever since participating in Senator Gore's failed campaign in 1970, I had been interested in politics. On election night in November 1980, I settled back in my recliner to find out whether President Carter would be re-elected or would be unseated by Ronald Reagan. By the time the night was over, I did not give a damn who our next president would be.

That night, Judy confronted me with the knowledge that she knew that I was having an affair. She also knew the identity of the "other woman." I knew it would do no good to deny it. The only question was, "What happens now?" I really expected to find myself "out in the street." But, Judy was practical and not willing to give up on her marriage so easily. I could stay, if only for the sake of our daughters. However, looking into Judy's eyes, I could see the disillusionment with the man she had once loved and admired but who had proven to be untrustworthy. When trust is gone, what remains? I knew things would never be the same between us. I realized that my dream of spending the rest of my life with Judy was only an illusion. It was only a matter of time before we would go our separate ways. But, for the time being, we both found it advantageous to maintain the status quo. To everyone else, we still had a "perfect marriage." We both found it expedient to maintain this façade.

Prelude to Disaster

Ever since the Marie Ragghianti case ended in July 1978, my life had gone smoothly as far as work was concerned. For the next two years, my work primarily consisted only of routine supervision of audits of state agencies, something I could do "standing on my head." I had occasional periods of depression but these incidents usually lasted less than two weeks. One reason that I had not had the "big one" was that for several years I had been under the care of a psychiatrist who was willing to do everything within his power to prevent another "meltdown." He knew of my mental history and the delicate nature of my psyche. He was willing to give me any medications necessary to keep me functional. When an "incident" occurred, I would run, not walk, to Dr. Brown for help. He adjusted my medications often to address the problem at hand. I came to admire Dr. Brown and rely on his kindness and understanding.

After the Ragghianti case was resolved by the courts, I decided that I did not want to work for Mr. Snodgrass anymore. However, I was not about to quit in a huff. I had decided to make state government my career choice and I was not going to let anything change my resolve. As soon as Governor Blanton left office in January 1979, and was replaced by Lamar Alexander, I began looking around for comparable positions in the executive branch. Given my present salary level, it was very difficult to find such a position.

However, during the years 1979 and 1980, on two different occasions, I had offers of employment from two different state agencies. Both times, the offers for employment were mysteriously withdrawn. I later found out through the grapevine that Mr. Greathouse had convinced the two agencies to withdraw the offers. When I later found this out I was furious. How dare he? I became even more determined than ever to leave. I would just bide my time until another position became open. Then I would confront Mr. Greathouse.

I had always heard "hindsight is better than foresight by a good sight." Now I know it is true. Although, at the time I was furious with Mr. Greathouse, I now know that he had my best interest at heart. He realized that any new employer might not be as understanding of my emotional and mental proclivities as was he. He was, in effect, protecting me from my own unwise decisions. As long as I was in his employ, I had a "safe harbor." Who knows what awaited me if I left. Nevertheless, at the time, I did not understand this. I just kept my eyes open for any opportunity to leave.

The fall of 1980 was a bad time for me. My world was caving in. Not only was my marriage in jeopardy and my job status in limbo, but I lost my "crutch," my psychiatrist, Dr. Brown. For years, I had run to Dr. Brown each time I faced a crisis, but otherwise, normally saw him only every three months. In the fall of 1980, I went to see Dr. Brown on one of my regularly scheduled visits, having last seen him three months before. I was shocked. He was emaciated. Seeing the bewilderment on my face, he explained that he had cancer of the esophagus. He didn't have to tell me that he was near death. From his appearance, that was obvious. Understandably, we did not discuss my problems that day. He just gave me the names of two psychiatrists. I left his office shaken. Would a new doctor be as understanding and supportive as Dr. Brown? I could only hope.

I randomly made my choice between the two doctors whose names Dr. Brown had given me without any investigation into their reputations. I just took it on faith that Dr. Brown would not lead me astray. What a big mistake. I know not what the doctor that I did not choose would have been like. I only know that the doctor I did choose proved to be a disaster. Appropriately, I will henceforth refer to him as Dr. Quack.

On my first visit to Dr. Quack, he was horrified at the both the quantity and nature of the medications that I was at that time taking. It did not take me long to ascertain that he was a psychiatrist who did not believe in antidepressants. Obviously, he thought that all depression was a result of conflicts a patient was having in their life. When he found out the problems that I was having in my marriage and my unfulfilled desire to change jobs, he jumped to the conclusion that these conflicts in my life were the cause of any depression I was experiencing. How could any competent psychiatrist ignore the history of depression in my family and my "meltdowns" in 1963, 1967 and 1969?

I should have walked out the door after the first visit. But foolishly, I did not. Like a fool, I continued going to him for over a year. Although he thought the medications that I was taking were vastly excessive and unnecessary, he reluctantly let me continue to take them. Each time that I visited him, about once every couple of months, he would threaten to discontinue the prescription for the medications. To me, they were my lifeline. I would plead with him not to "cut me off," sometimes resorting to crying. Reluctantly, he would patronize me and agree to my continuing to take the medications. I should have realized that eventually he would lose his patience with me. He would eventually become fed up and cut me off. What would I do then? I tried not to think about it.

Decision Time

During the fall of 1981, decisions would be made that would alter my life forever. My marriage was continuing to "go south." I was working for a man, Mr. Snodgrass, for whom I had lost respect. I was hanging by a thread with a psychiatrist who obviously thought me a "nut case." I could not live like this. A "normal" person would have had trouble surviving this trauma. With my mental and emotional baggage, I felt another "meltdown" was probably inevitable. What could I do to avoid such a fate?

In 1969, I had erroneously thought that going back to Charlotte would be a "cure all" for my problems. Of course, it was not and ended in disaster. Nevertheless I now somehow rationalized that if I could now only get a "fresh start" in a new job, everything else would fall into place. All my problems would melt away. Desperation often leads to irrational thinking. When in late September 1981, a position opened up in the Department of Education at a comparable salary to the salary I was then making, I immediately applied for the position. This time, Mr. Greathouse, rather than opposing my leaving State Audit, helped me secure the position. I do not know whether or not he thought I had finally conquered my depression or was just tired of "babysitting" me, protecting me from myself. At any rate, I got the job. It was decided that I would assume my new position January 1, 1982, giving me time to tie up loose ends with regard to ongoing audits in State Audit. Little did I realize how much can happen in three short months.

In November another decision was made that brought me to my knees. It was not a decision of mine but that of Dr. Quack. He had decided, at last, to severely cut back my medications. I begged, pleaded, cried and threw myself on his mercy. It was all to no avail. He was tired of putting up with me. He had made a decision and would stick to it. Had I been thinking rationally, I would have told him to go to hell and found another psychiatrist who understood that depression is often caused by a chemical imbalance in the brain. Instead, I abided by his decision. I left his office thinking that I had no other options than to try and "tough it out."

At first, I thought that I would be alright. It took a couple of weeks for the medication to get out of my system. However, by the middle of December, I realized that I was in the middle of yet another "meltdown." Like had happened in prior "meltdowns," I could not concentrate or focus on anything. My mind was "mush." Not only was I severely depressed, I realized that in two weeks I would start a new job. I could not possibly function in a new job. What was I to do? Everything seemed so hopeless. Just when I thought things could not get any worse, they did. A few days before I was to report to my new job, I had a panic attack, the first of several that I would have to endure.

Through the years, I have heard many people who claimed to have had panic attacks. Most of these people have no idea of what actually constitutes a panic attack. There is a big difference in anxiety and panic. A couple of days after Christmas when I had my first panic attack, I was relaxing one night, sitting in my recliner, when I dozed off. When I awoke, I was in a panic. I aimlessly raced upstairs as fast as I could. Once upstairs, without reason, I began desperately feeling first the floor, then the walls. This went on for several minutes. Finally, utterly exhausted, I rolled over on my back hyperventilating. This episode scared the hell out of me. My depression had entered into yet another dimension. Where would it all end? And yet, a few days later, knowing I could not function, I was to report to the Commissioner of Education to assume my new duties.

Descent into Hell

When the time came for me to report for my new job with the Department of Education on January 1, 1982, I felt like a condemned man. I knew that I was nearing the end of my rope. I was worse off than in 1969, before the "Escape to Nowhere." At least, while working for the CPA firm in '69, I was fairly adept at hiding my depression by just "faking it." Now I suspected that my days of faking it were about over. But somehow I had to carry on, day by day, as long as I could.

I first met with the Commissioner of Education, my boss, who seemed pleased to see me. I now suspect that he had hired me because he probably felt that by hiring an experienced employee of State Audit, it would be easier to keep Mr. Greathouse at bay. Surely, Mr. Greathouse would rely on one of his former supervisors to keep the department on the straight and narrow. Maybe now Mr. Greathouse would stay out of the Commissioner's hair.

After my introduction to the Commissioner and a tour of the department's administrative offices, I was shown my new office, such as it was. It was, in fact, just a "cubbyhole," far removed from the Commissioner's Office and the other administrative offices. Normally, I would have been irate about being so far removed from anything having to do with the fiscal operations of the department. But, I was anything but normal. I felt it a blessing to be so far removed from daily operations. The less contact I had with anyone, the better.

I was also lucky in that I had only one auditor who reported to me. Although having only two auditors in an operation the size of the Department of Education was a joke, it was a blessing in disguise. The department's other auditor, Jack Parker, was a real "go-getter" used to setting his own agenda. I did not have to worry about Jack being a problem, or so I thought. He was content "doing his own thing."

The first two or three weeks, I actually tried to do something useful to carry out my assigned mission. I had brought all kinds of audit materials from State Audit to help me in starting an audit plan. But I knew it was hopeless. Most of the time, I just stared blankly out into space, oblivious of my surroundings. Only when someone entered my office did I "snap out of it" and try to have a normal conversation. Jack, desiring to get to know me and also needing assistance on one of his projects, suggested that I accompany him on a three- or four-city tour gathering information for a report he was writing. Reluctantly, I agreed, wondering how much help I would be. The trip was to commence in about a week.

Before I left on this trip with Jack, I decided to take one last desperate attempt to save both my sanity and my job. I knew that this "meltdown" had been precipitated by Dr. Quack's refusing to continue to give me the antidepressants I so desperately needed. I was through with Dr. Quack. I would no longer plead with him or throw myself on his mercy. Maybe another psychiatrist would see my plight and help me. A friend of mine, who had been helped by Dr. Steven Nyquist, suggested that I see him. Fortunately, I was able to get an immediate appointment with Dr. Nyquist, before I was to take my trip with Jack.

The difference between Dr. Nyquist and Dr. Quack was like the difference between daylight and dark. Dr. Nyquist, after sympathetically hearing my life's story, suggested that I take a series of psychological tests, which I did. After analyzing the tests, Dr. Nyquist was very blunt: "You are a severely depressed young man, but I think I can help you." My spirits rebounded. I left his office not only with a prescription for an antidepressant that I had never taken before but a renewed hope that I would, at last, be alright. I rushed to the pharmacy, got the prescription filled, and immediately took my first dose right there in the pharmacy. Like so many people after taking a new medicine, I immediately felt better. That night, I felt like a new man. I was saved at last.

The next morning, when I awoke, I came back down to earth. I was just as depressed as before. How irrational must have been my thought process to think one dose would turn my life around. It was a case of too little, too late. The "meltdown" was too far along. There was no hope for me. I left the following Monday on the three-day trip around the state with Jack. I said almost nothing on the trip. I had given up "faking it." I did not give a damn anymore what happened to me. When we got back from the trip, Jack "called me out." "You were no help. What's wrong with you? You need help." I did not respond. I just gathered my things, walked out the door, went home and climbed into bed.

I would have liked to have stayed in bed forever. No more "faking it." No more worries. I did not give a damn what happened to me. I am not sure how many days I stayed in bed.

My wife, of course, was beside herself. What could she do? What should she do? She tried to coax me to join the family in the living room. Her attempts were to no avail. She pleaded with me incessantly, trying to convince me to go see Dr. Nyquist. Even though I felt my life was over and that no one could help me, finally, after several days, I reluctantly agreed to see Dr. Nyquist.

I was disheartened when I got to Dr. Nyquist's office to find that he would be out of town for a couple of days. His associate, whose name I recall but will not disclose, was seeing Dr. Nyquist's patients in addition to his own. As it so happens, when I arrived, late in the afternoon, I was the only patient in the waiting room. The walls to the doctors' offices were not as soundproof as they should have been. I heard the doctor say to his nurse: "What's wrong with this turkey anyway?" Had I been myself, I would have stormed out of the office in righteous indignation. But, I was so desperate I just sat there with my humiliation. What difference did it make anyway? Finally, I was called into the doctor's office. I could not stop crying as I told him of my desperate plight. He stated the obvious. I needed to be in a psychiatric hospital. He called the hospital and made the arrangements for my admission. At last, I would be where I belonged.

A New Day

It was February 1982 when I entered the private psychiatric hospital, a bleak month for everyone but especially for me. In truth, I was so withdrawn from reality and the world that I remember very little about the first few weeks I was there. I do remember that for the first couple of days the staff more or less observed my conduct to get a read on the severity of my problem. Perhaps this is standard operating procedure or perhaps they were just waiting for Dr. Nyquist to return. I did have the presence of mind to tell them that I never wanted to see that SOB associate ever again. (Dr. Nyquist, soon thereafter, disassociated himself from this heartless clown.)

I was very easy for the staff to observe. Just as I had at home, I spent as much time as possible in my bed. I would go to the eating area for my meals but would set a speed record gobbling them down, so that I could return to my bed once more. As I had done my last few days at home, I would lie there trying to convince myself that I had not "lost my mind," that I was not insane. I had a fantastic memory of my past. I would lie there and remember everything that I had ever done, no matter how insignificant, from my earliest memory until my entry into the hospital. When finished, I would start all over again. If I could reconstruct my whole life, that meant I was still sane? Didn't it?

After Dr. Nyquist arrived on the scene, a couple of days later, my days of lying in bed were over. Even though I had no interest in the activities he prescribed, Dr. Nyquist insisted that I get involved. Along with the other patients, I had walks on the hospital grounds, even though it was the dead of winter and we all had to wear coats. There were projects in crafts. I had always hated crafts since my days at summer camp when I was twelve years old, but I had no choice, I was forced to participate. There were classes in aerobics and other physical routines. On occasion, we would go bowling. There were also groups where all patients were encouraged to discuss their problems. The whole program involved keeping the patients active while their doctors determined the roots of each individual's problems.

It did not take Dr. Nyquist long, after analyzing my past, to decide that although I definitely had issues in my marriage and work, my history would indicate that my depression was not brought about by life's problems but by a chemical imbalance in my brain. Before Dr. Nyquist had time to decide the proper medication to prescribe for me, I had yet another panic attack, where I ran up and down the hospital corridor, feeling the walls and floors in a panic. The challenge for Dr. Nyquist was to find a medication, or combination thereof, that would address both my propensity for depression and my tendency to have panic attacks. He finally put me on a combination of medications that he felt would address both problems. However, he warned me that I should not expect immediate relief. It might take several weeks before he could determine if this combination of medications was, indeed, addressing the problem. In the meantime, I could only hope and pray.

As the weeks went by, I came to realize the vast difference in this hospital and the state hospital which I had voluntarily entered in 1969. The people in this hospital, for sure had serious problems. However, each patient had something lacking in the state hospital, hope. I could not help but recall the "hopeless souls" from 1969 or the role my "Mother Teresa," Dr. Vorbusch, had played in returning me to society and a semblance of normalcy. Now, could Dr, Nyquist do the same thing?

After a few weeks, I was encouraged that I had had no further panic attacks. However, I remained deeply depressed. One day, several members of the staff, when encountering me, smiled and said how good I looked and congratulated me on my being better. I was furious. I felt no better. I remained deeply depressed. Was this a ploy by Dr. Nyquist to trick me? When Dr. Nyquist came by that day, as he did every day, I let him have it with both barrels. After I had accused him of trickery and deception, he only smiled and informed me that there was no deception involved. I really did look better. Apparently, there was a sparkle in my eye that was not there before. He thought that I had "turned the corner."

Sure enough, in a couple of days I experienced a glimmer of hope. Thereafter, instead of dreading waking up each morning, I could not wait for the next day to come. Each day I felt better and better. I had been treated with antidepressants in the past, but always, they had been only a temporary relief, followed by, at best, "mini-episodes" instead of "meltdowns." I had always been waiting for the "other shoe to fall." I somehow knew that this time was different. For once I had confidence that my life was just beginning, not ending as I had always feared. During April, Dr, Nyquist, realizing that, at last, I was free from depression, released me from the hospital.

My first night home, I went out on the deck at the rear of our home. It was a dark night. The moon and starts showed brightly in the sky. As I had done so often in the past, I thought of the words of Samuel Taylor Coleridge in the poem: "Dejection: An Ode," where he described his own depression, with which I had always been able to relate:

A grief without a pang, void, dark, and drear
A stifled, drowsy, unimpassioned grief,
Which finds no natural outlet, no relief.

Mr. Coleridge described his viewing of the moon and stars while depressed this way:

Those stars, that glide behind them or between,
Now sparkling, now bedimmed, but always seen
Yon crescent Moon, as fixed as if it grew
In its own cloudless, starless lake of blue
I see them all so excellently fair,
I see, not feel, how beautiful they are!

That night, as I looked up at the moon and stars, I began to weep, not out of depression or sadness but out of joy. For the first time in my life, as I gazed at the heavens, I not only saw but FELT how beautiful they were!

Epilogue

I am now sixty-four years old and have lived going on twenty-five years depression-free. Since my "meltdown" in 1982, I have faced many trials and tribulations. I have fared no better or worse than others in facing life's challenges. However, at least, I have been able to make my decisions, for better or worse, with a clear mind, free from the debilitating effects of depression. Any significance to my life cannot be measured by any accomplishments, or lack thereof in my life. The only thing that distinguishes my life from others is the demons of depression I was forced to fight the first thirty-nine years of my life. Many have fought similar battles and lost. I am one of the lucky ones. I survived.

I would be remiss if I left the reader hanging, not knowing how I have fared since 1982. I will give a short synopsis of my life since that time. Not surprisingly, a week after I returned home from the hospital in April, Judy asked me for a divorce. I am sure she would have done so long before; however, being such a nice person, she refused to kick me when I was down. My daughters, Shannon and Melanie, have grown up to be fine young women who love both Judy and me very much. Judy remarried and now lives in Kentucky. In the spring of 1983, Mary Margaret Kendrick and I were married. After a long search, I had at last found the love of my life. We have been happily married twenty-four years. Shannon and Melanie have come to love and admire Mary Margaret.

In spite of an inauspicious beginning of my employment by the Department of Education, the officials of the department were very understanding and supportive of me during those very trying times. I worked in the department for twenty-two years before retiring in January 2004. Counting my eleven years service with the State Comptroller's Office, I worked for the state for thirty-three years. I owe everything that I have achieved during my tenure with the state to Bill White, who gave me a chance in those dark days when no one else would.

But life is not a fairytale. There are always bumps in the road. In 1983, I experienced yet another one. Dr. Nyquist, impressed with how well I had been doing, decided to adjust my medications by putting me on an antidepressant with less potential long-term side effects than the medication that I was on. I soon found myself suffering depression once again. Dr. Nyquist immediately put me back on my original combination of medications. This time, I knew it was just a matter of time before the medications "kicked in." In good time, they did. It was obvious that I would have to take these medications for the rest of my life. To this day, I have been taking those original medications every day, and with no discernable side effects.

My experience with depression has resulted in my being much more tolerant and forgiving of the frailties of other people. Because I know what it is like to hit "rock bottom," I am probably more tolerant of the downtrodden than most. I am sure that each homeless person has a tragic story to tell. Who would choose to lead the life of a homeless person unless life was too terrible to endure? Many of those shunned and looked down on are mentally ill. When I see a homeless person with that blank far away stare, a look of hopelessness in their eyes, it is like looking in a mirror. It is all I can do to keep from weeping. For I know that there but for the grace of God go I.

My mother died in January 1996. My father lived until his early eighties, dying in August 2005. I have heard it said that when a man's father dies, he is forced to face his own mortality. That is certainly true in my case. At sixty-four, I now find that what once were my long-term goals are now, by necessity, my short-term goals. My main goal, and the purpose of this book, is to let people know that depression can be overcome. There are presently multitudes of persons struggling to get through each day, living empty lives, knowing only hopelessness and despair. If only a handful of the depressed seek help as a result of this book, my life will not have been lived in vain.

When I was in college, like many college students, I became an agnostic. As I have matured and observed the vastness and order of the universe and the wonder of life itself, I now know that there is an omnipotent creative force responsible for the creation, yes, a God. Yet I shun organized religion, preferring a direct, personal relationship with my God. I am a Deist. Like most reasoning men who think for themselves, I sometimes have doubts about the possibility of an afterlife. And yet, when my thoughts turn negative, I always remember the following lines from "In Memoriam" by Tennyson, first learned in Mrs. Cook's class in Central High School:

Thou wilt not leave us in the dust:
Thou madest man, he knows not why,
He thinks he was not made to die;
And thou hast made him: thou art just.